THE STRUCTURE OF DESTRUCTION: PART II
THE WALLS COME TRUE

Douglas Messerli

THE WALLS COME TRUE
An Opera for Spoken Voices

THE STRUCTURE OF DESTRUCTION: PART II

○

○

○

○

○

SUN & MOON PRESS
LOS ANGELES • 1995

This edition first published in paperback in 1996 by Littoral Books

10 9 8 7 6 5 4 3 2 1

FIRST EDITION

Selections from this volume previously appeared in *From the Other Side of the Century:
A New American Poetry 1960–1990* (Los Angeles: Sun & Moon Press, 1994)
and in *New Directions 55: An International Anthology of
Prose & Poetry* (New York: New Directions, 1991)

Cover: Roberto Barni, *Meriggio,* 1986
Reprinted by permission of the artist
Design: Katie Messborn
Typography: Guy Bennett

LIBRARY OF CONGRESS CATALOGING IN PUBLICATION DATA
Messerli, Douglas [1947]
The Walls Come True: An Opera for Spoken Voices
p. cm
ISBN: 1-55713-180-5
I. Title. II. Author
811'.54—dc20

Printed in the United States of America on acid-free paper.

for David Antin

This work was first produced in its entirety by the Los Angeles Theater of the Ear in collaboration with The Contemporary Arts Educational Project, Inc. at *Beyond Baroque Foundation,* January 25, 1991. Directed by Paul Vangelisti; Sound by Ed Hammond.

CAST

VOICES

    Anne Gee Byrd
    Robert Crosson
    Diana Daves
    Bill Hunt
    John C. McLaughlin

ANNOUNCER

    Beata Pozniak

Act I and the Entr'acte [Twelve Tyrants Between Acts; or Mundane Moments in Insane Histories] was first performed at St. Mark's Church in the Bowery in 1989 with the following cast:

VOICES

    Charles Bernstein
    Len Jenkin
    Nick Piombino
    Fiona Templeton
    Mac Wellman

ANNOUNCER

    Douglas Messerli

The same sections were performed at the University of California, San Diego in La Jolla in 1990 with the following performers:

VOICES
    David Antin
    Michael Davidson
    Jerome Rothenberg
    Diane Rothenberg
    Pasquale Verdicchio
ANNOUNCER
    Douglas Messerli

Complete darkness, an enveloping blanket so thick one might smother ## ACT I

◗ *Letters appear upon the light board:*
THE QUIET WOMAN

Blue light surrounds a speaker, woman or man.

To start at the beginning you must walk away from where you have begun. Although she never struck her mother, father, neighbor, cat, dog, or brother, and seldom spoke, and when she did "find" her voice it was held at the level of a whisper ("a purr" as a family member put it), she was described as being violent in the end. Was her silence a sign of hate? Is intercourse at war with war? It is said that Napoleon could talk your head off.

◗ *Letters upon the light board:*
SEXUAL REVOLUTION

A spot focuses upon another.

The point is dangerous, to plant the barb without regretting it. I mean I could have killed her I was so mad. Is anger a hyperbole for murder? Or does the exaggeration lie in the slap that turned into a stroke? Was she a striking woman, I mean the kind of beauty that might make men desire to grab her and possess? What they call a bomb-shell with a couple of cannons for breasts?

Simultaneously a film or projected video behind the figure speaking represents a woman pulling a Nazi soldier into an alleyway. Her laughing face pulls his nearer yet to kiss.

▷ *Letters upon the light board:*
THE SAVAGE

Woman at the apron

Imagine a man who is not yet beast. Who does not comprehend the relation of the sun to the surface of his birth. How can we talk about something like that, of a history before it has begun? Of a mystery with neither clue nor solution? The detective was having breakfast in the garden when the gardener suddenly shot stark naked out of the bush. He didn't have an alibi, a tongue so it seemed, or a sense of having wandered into the plot.

The detective took his gun from its holster. But the thing just ran, not for its life but for the pleasure of it. Or what we imagined was pleasure, the air rushing round the cheeks upper and lower both. Indeed the detective was aroused by this and went running after the beauty discovered by the dick.

▷ *Letters upon the light board:*
SILENCE

What is silence? Is it the absence or control of the voice? When we speak of a voice in a poem does that mean we "hear" it or that there is a pattern or patter there that is so

8

particular that we can identify it as belonging to the air? Then it is not the same as a good eye in art or a good ear in music or a good leg on an opening night. For it exists not in the possessor but in the possessed.

Simultaneously with the above speech a dancer takes the center of the stage, standing in the middle of her spot. A male joins her. She takes his hand in hers, cradles it, and begins to rock. Higher and higher they swing until his fist rubs her jaw. She draws back.

● *Letters upon the light board*:
IN A PINCH

A man to the left

To rub the palm against a cheek is traditional in ancient tribes as an expression of admiration or love. A female dancer stands in the middle of her spot, taking the male dancer's hand in hers to cradle it, rocking back and forth until he gets into the swing. As the arc grows ever higher and higher he reaches her jaw when she suddenly checks the action and holds his hand in place. The woman who sits beside me asks "Is she supposed to be expecting?" I tell her the Italians do it best.

● *Letters upon the light board*:
SILENCE AGAIN

The same or another man

I once saw *Persona* and didn't understand. An actress decided never to speak again. And another woman came to live with her or maybe she was there at the beginning.

And they had what seemed to be a lesbian affair. But of course it may have been that they were the same person or nearly identical twins or reverse images of each other. I think everyone recognized that. But what was Bergman saying all my friends asked. And I couldn't answer.

Film or projected video simultaneously portrays a seated man in utter silence lectured to, verbally abused by a strutting one. Behind the man stands a woman verbalizing the emotions of the silent one.

 ● *Letters upon the light board*:
THE TEXT

A woman comes forth.

If a text is a structure of an utterance, its context is what washes up with the waves. A pencil, a hat pin, a nail hammered (by the sea) from a human hand, a container of —water now, the boots you are in. So if I ask "who done it?" are you prepared to sort through this and other matter in search of something someone else might have missed? Was the pin perhaps topped with pearl, the rubber of a boot pierced with the pin, the barrel bearing oysters? Put anything into it and your guess is correct. The pencil writes the hat.

Complete blackout

● *Letters upon the light board*:
HOPE

A voice

Behind blindness there is consciousness still. The dreamer has his dream, the infirmed the informing pain and possible recovery. The senile have spells in which they can recall the colors of their childhood dress. The comatose, they say, register the comings and goings of family and friends in micrometric movements of the mouth. Oh, but the dead!

A moment's pause, the rhythm of a gulp, a rest

● *Letters upon the light board*:
THE PRESENT

Full light reveals several figures traveling in haste.
A woman speaks on the run.

The aim of the present is to get it over with. The now is the sacred cow of the moment, desperate to be milked. Drink and you enter the diary. Abstain and it ruptures the past, becoming what you have at stake.

○ *Letters upon the light board*:
HATE

A man momentarily stops.

Today I told my lover of my hate. Hurt, he kissed my honesty and left me alone with the uncertainty that I had spoken the truth. I had planned it out, practiced some of my words in order to produce the proper effect. But I had not prepared myself for the result: in his tears, I loved him, licking his wounds.

○ *Letters upon the light board*:
THE CAT

A gossip cannot resist.

As a cat. That was how she thought she had come back. In Egypt, in the court of Tutankhamen, she was kept by a Princess whose name understandably she had forgotten at this late date. But she remembered a patio, a sort of porch with palms and plates of olives and a couch that sounded like something Cecille B. De Mille might create. A Nubian perhaps? Never! In her current life she was from Georgia and wouldn't hear of having "a black" to wait on her whims. That was how she had come to be so different from her kinfolk. Having lived in Thebes had opened her up to all sorts of experiences that they would never even imagine. For instance, she had laid on many laps.

◗ *Letters upon the light board*:
THE FOX

The pedant lectures.

I am interested in the way words begin to get where they are going, not where they have gone. Dead ears do not define the desires of the farmer's son sowing his seed as he may. The end is naturally a den where the fox is trapped by snapping hounds. But at the sound of the horn who can say where the beasts will be led. Less for cleverness than for survival's sake—the reason as well why storytellers seldom take the simple path through a paragraph—the indefinite noun we seek may be embedded in the clause, come running out and confuse us with the shift of the subordinate, pause, return to the topic at hand and rhyme its way away the way a lay usually ends up. There they are—she so hot on his little red tail that for a second it seems to the bitch the first shall be forced to submit. Then away they dart, not about some Middlesex mansion with the rich on their heels, but out of a field of Kansas corn where you seldom see horses and dogs are kept to barn and house.

◗ *Letters upon the light board*:
ECONOMICS

A student explains his past.

She was very poor and I was very rich. Or shall I say I was richer than she was poor. Or perhaps she was poorer than she presented herself and I was richer yet. Or I, wanting to impress, exaggerated just a little being poorer than I presented myself. It all depends upon economics. She was perhaps less poor than any man in Pakistan, which by contrast made her very rich; and I less rich than the people in Afghanistan, if by rich you understand what is meant by religious men. But I had enough. And she never did seem to have anything, even though she often had something in her purse. I had a credit card, but I had to be careful in its use. It would be embarrassing, for example, if after dinner I put the card onto the platter and it came back with apologies from the waiter who had been told by American Express that I no longer had credit with them, which would mean, obviously, that I didn't have money to pay the check. But as I said, I never had to worry. She always had cash.

On film or projected video a man lectures buried up to his neck in sand.

○ *Letters upon the light board*:
THE OLD WIVES' TALE

A priest stops to talk.

It is said if you bury a rhubarb stalk under the moon–the best is a full one–and sprinkle chalk in a circle under the sun at noon upon the same spot you'll be married by May and divorced the same night.

○ *Letters on the light board*:
ROCKS AND CLOCKS

An artist interrupts.

There is always another way to tell the same story. For example, I have a friend who collects rocks. She has thousands of rocks, not only on tables, shelves, and mantels where people might normally display them, and on every window ledge, but in beds and chairs, in closets and shoes and in the icebox. Naturally people think this is strange and so they keep their distance. Which is really too bad, because my friend in every other way is very normal, kind, and generous to a fault. If you were sick and couldn't get to the physician's, she'd run you over in a second. She'd clean your house if you let her. She'd bake a cake—although she'd always burn it—and take you over a hot plate.

I have another friend who collects clocks. He has them on the mantel too, and on shelves and tables and in closets and odd corners here and there. But no one seems to think there's anything unusual in that. People are always over at his place. Which is rather strange really because he isn't very nice. Right in the middle of a conversation he'll walk out of the room and start tinkering away on one or another of his cuckoos. And even if you're absolutely parched he won't ever offer a glass of ice. And yet people come from miles around to see him and to hear all those ticking clocks strike.

One day I thought about this for hours. Why should people prefer clocks to rocks? Or look one way at one and another at the other? Both are created from little pieces, bits, of intricate metal in the one and in the other of sand and dust. Both tell us of time: the first by the second, the second by the age. And both will wear down if you wait long enough: the metal will fatigue and rust in the clock, wind and water will disintegrate the rock.

Despite these similarities, however, there are essential differences. The one is all noise in motion, the other suspension, silence. And while the one is all man-made, the other has nothing at all to do with us. In short, the one is naturally why the other is art.

Only then did I comprehend the intense hostility between the yard and the house.

On film a man puts a monocle into place, removes it, and enters a café.

◐ *Letters upon the light board:*
ADVANCED CIVILIZATION

The philosopher concludes.

The surest signifier of an advanced civilization is a culture's willingness to convert, cut away, tear down, or blow itself up. By contrast, primitive societies—even the nomadic—investing the structures which provide their protection with value (*la qualité*)—anthropormorphize, humanize, and ultimately sanctify the constructions in which they work and play.

All actions stop.

Letters upon the light board:
CORPUS DELICTI

The undertaker eulogizes.

There are three characteristics of a corpse: pallor, permanence, and putrification. Contrary to popular opinion, however, in its hiss of tissue falling in upon the bones it is neither motionless nor mute.

16

○ *Letters upon the light board*:
SUMMER

Chorus

All afternoon the sun hides summer, the way such really bright things stand between what actually is and what might be if we could truly treat each day as a freshly washed window. (Fortunately, we have clean forgotten to, so that the smears of oil we traced with our childhood fingers across the rain-rivuletted deposits of yearly dust blur our vision and we see secondarily what we might have witnessed at first as a self-reflection.) They come back, not even hauntingly, since that would imply some vague recognition of a past we now understand only as a future desire to be as young as we think we might have been then—come right into the room where we sit waiting, strangers to us alone. We want to cry, "Stay!" But all we can do is shiver.

> *In a dumbshow two people walk the street, meet, appear to recognize one another, think better, walk away.*
> *Reality disappears with the people on the street.*
> *Light becomes softer, nostalgic.*

○ *Letters upon the light board*:
FICTION

The storyteller sits upon a stool, very high in the air.

The detective opened his book to an imaginary page. It was there all right, but the detective didn't care, wanting to appear as if he were a student of fiction. And so, he imagined what might have been on the page had he the inclination to look down upon it.

He saw a tall woman, dressed to the gills, who stared haughtily at him as she passed. What reason did she have to be in the garden? And why would anyone on a hot day like this want to wear fox? Things didn't read right. Why did the nurse with long black lashes have a dog on her lap? And why was the gardener pointing his hose to the trees instead of to grass? According to the news it was supposed to be cloudy, a chance of rain perhaps.

○ *Letters upon the light board:*
HOME

The man as a Romantic

When I was ten my parents betrayed me, sending their only son away to a Swiss pensionat. For many months I was confused—unable to comprehend how they could get along without me—angry and homesick on alternating days. For misbehaving in one of my classes—I have no memory of the crime anymore—I was called to the headmaster's and sternly commanded to begin packing since I was going back. I could not believe my ears, and in absolute shock retorted, "I've just been sent away! How can I return to them?" The rector grimly assured me, "We'll call and arrange it with your father." "My father is dead," I lied. "Your mother then. We'll call your mother." "Oh, you mustn't..." I stammered, my imagination out of control, "for then she'll never be able to marry again. With a problem like me on her hands, it's impossible for her to get someone to tie the knot."

The headmaster shook his head in distress. "Yes. Yes, that explains everything, your behavior with the other boys and such. Return to Grammar!"

From that moment forward I no longer cared for my family—if you understand caring the way children are convinced that instead of being a product of their parents, their elders have been assigned to them. For suddenly I comprehended that instead of being upheld as a haven a home could be presented as a punishment. And the truth could take you there without an explanation.

Besides, within the year my father really did die, of a heart attack, and my mother remarried his partner in the firm. And I was asked to abandon the institution I had come to love.

Film of a man cornering a boy, querying, lecturing, and kissing him.

❍ *Letters upon the light board:*
THE BEACH

The man, also sitting on such a stool, recalls a strange event.

My wife and I went to the beach where we witnessed a man lying in the sand, not as others, sprawled upon it frying in the sun, but with head and hands appearing only, he preached to us of our sins. A little crowd gathered round him, some to jeer, a few to applaud, a couple to kick sand in his face which had gotten very red in the heat and the excitement of what he said. "Come out of there!" the lifeguard called over. "I can't," he paused in his list of our transgressions, "until everyone here has knelt in prayer." A boy collapsed to his knees and began to beat his breast in mockery. "Gawd, forgive me!" "He's a loony!" another man shouted, shielding his eyes from the sun to see the buried priest better. Several in attendance walked off as if they suddenly remembered that they had come out to celebrate the day, and wandering out of reach of his message they laid down blankets and bodies upon them. Some stayed to taunt his torsoless rantings, but becoming bored, most of these also fell away. Two boys alone stayed to keep up the banter, racing round and round the plot until one tripped his friend who pulled the first to ground with him.

"Sit down," my wife commanded. "The lifeguard has gone to get a shovel."

● *Letters upon the light board*:
THE BUS

The woman in a similar position tells a story too.

At sixteen she struck out on her own, tired of taking orders from the restauranteur for whom she was busing in return for board. At the café he insisted that she be always punctual, but at home he and his wife didn't care when she arrived or departed—as long as she showered with lava and lathered her hair before entering their presence since she smelled otherwise of burgers. But basically they were good middle-class shopkeeping folk, fat and friendly with their friends, scowling and suspicious only to those who they didn't know better than to say hello. Yet she wouldn't give them the time of day, and wasn't there most of the time to tell them. She was working—mornings, noons, nights, Saturdays, after church Sundays. How much could a bed cost? She stopped by the hotel to ask and got a reputation for coming out. Suddenly she was struck with the realization that she had to get out of town now or go out of her mind later. Then she was suddenly in a hurry to catch the bus; she couldn't miss it. But since she was a little bored and now had something to live up to, she stopped to say hello to the boy who did her dirty dishes.

● *Letters upon the light board*:
THE LONGEST DAY

A young man infatuated with his own thoughts

I seek always a history for what lies outside of it. For example, how do we measure the days of the creation? Since man was not permitted to come into existence until the sixth we can assume that those days before us were not the same as those by which we now measure that short distance between our death and birth. And since we believe that animals cannot calculate, let alone perceive the spinning motions of our planet round the sun, we can presume that Moses spoke of days in God's eyes, which for us could be centuries, eons, a time longer that anything we might even contemplate. And since it seems quite inconsistent to change context in that very same verse, the seventh "day," the one on which God rests, as far as we're concerned may still be taking place—which would explain why humankind has had some difficulties on this earth.

► *Letters upon the light board*:
TO THE POET

The lightboard prints sentences:
THE PEOPLE ARE STARVING FOR LANGUAGE. POET, CARVE YOUR SOUL! LEAVE THE FISH TALE TO OTHERS.

► *Letters upon the light board*:
IT

The poet finally speaks, enthroned higher in the air yet.

They had carved their names in the tree, Irma and Thomas or Ilene and Thaddeus or Irina and Tobias—once upon a time I had dozens of names. But for me the tree had now one name only, a name I spoke all summer long. I am going to sit under IT, to read under IT, to sleep under IT, to dream perhaps. My parents understood IT as a pronoun only and were disturbed a bit by my continual usage of such a vague referent.

I dreamt that my uncle—a baker in Perpignan who described himself as "a poet in the pan"—came to us for a visit. Despite his presence I asked to be excused from the table that I might contemplate under IT for a spell. My uncle looked confused, and my father explained that I was going through a stage common to young men as they grow from the concrete cradle of their mother's hold into the abstract arms of the human race. My uncle laughed: "It is it is it?" And my parents took their turn with perplexity.

He recalled how one day his little shop had been visited by a heavyset American devotee of croissants. She was a poet as it turned out, and since he had always fancied himself also as one they began to chat. He had brought her sweets several times since that and grown rather fond of her and her friend. She had just such an aphorism, about roses he said. And turning to me again he called out "It is it is it?" And this time the whole room roared—although I don't think my father really understood what his humor was about.

I was embarrassed. Hurt. And when I got to IT I pulled off a low hanging branch. Later, when I awoke, I took out a knife, scraped away its initials, and put mine in their place.

○ *Letters upon the light board*:
RAISON

The first storyteller begins again.

In the corner of the garden the detective noticed that his favorite Quercus robur in the whole province had had a large quarter of its bark hacked out. "What," expostulated Mr. Reason, "can be the meaning of this? Who would punish such a grand pedunculata?" But before he could get his temper completely worked up, he was overcome with a wave of nostalgia so overwhelming that for the first time ever on the job he pondered his past.

He recalled how his father had once taken his brother and him out into the woods to see a tree under which they sat. The breeze blew the sunlight into ellipses on their laps. And he, a normally disconsolate lad, laughed.

"It's your tree, Charles," suddenly proclaimed his father. The child was taken aback: "Why is that?" "Because it has stolen the frown from your face, and because," continued the ordinarily taciturn pâtissier, "it has your initials on it." Tracing the point of his father's finger to the very bottom of the tree close down to its roots his eyes displayed delight in the discovery of those letters .

"What does it mean, papa?" he asked.

"It is the beginning of something, a word or a romance, which you alone can finish."

For days the child wandered the house brooding over every word which began with the letters upon which, it appeared, depended his fate. "Crisis? Crest? Crossroad? Crown! Cry? Crush? Credible? Crank. Cruise. Crude! Crucify? No. I shall change my name to Thomas."

Temporary blackout

● *Letters on the light board*:
THE TRIAL

A journalist reports.

The trial was set to begin in May, and everyone wanted a pass. Madame Croset wrote to the judge, and he wrote back: "It is out of my hands."

Spying the bedside note, her maid told the nanny who told a teacher who told her class that the French judicial system was completely corrupt. "Upon no evidence men make decisions," she wrote the Gazette which, in its next editorial, called for the dismissal of the judge.

On the day of his death, he wrote in a journal they found in a grasp rigor mortis had already set, "Madame has my permission to view the corpse."

Simultaneously projected slides or film of several trees, one of which has initials carved into it

❍ *Letters upon the light board*:
BONE

The philosopher strolls in.

When the French say *bon* we do not mean good the way the Americans might say "that's good!" advocating a betterment of the human race. For us it is closer to your bone, that thing the dog guardedly buries in memory of the meat upon it once. A kind of cut, but not cynical really, the way some Britishers might say "oh, goodie." We simply still have to chew awhile until it sinks into taste.

❍ *Letters upon the light board*:
THE PHILOSOPHER

Sentence upon the light board:
THE SEEKER OF TRUTH AND ITS POSSESSOR IS THE DIFFERENCE BE-
TWEEN A PHILOSOPHER AND THE COMMON MAN.

○ *Letters upon a blackboard*:
CR

The professor lectures, back turned to audience, as if the blackboard were his class.

Professor Fahrni has argued, convincingly I think, that these letters found throughout the province were originally C-R-S, the s generally unexpressed by the cult of early Christians at Perpignan because it was thought to be the devil's sign beginning as it did so many evil words such as snake, sin, and, of course, Satan. Based on that assumption we can interpret the letters as a reference to Christ the Risen Savior—the trinomial of the messiah through which members of the early church secretly expressed their faith. Some of these believers would have also perceived the cryptogram in its entirety as C R S

H I T, the savior's name read in rows instead of across as representing the Christ who bled (symbolized by the "read rows" or "red rose" manifest in the thorns of his crown) when flagellated ("hit") by Pilate's soldiers.

And for the most fervent of these believers who read this at angles (being the true "angels" of the early church) the sign would have been seen as

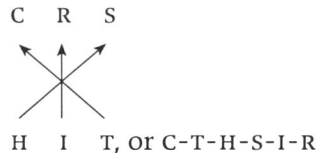

C   R   S

H   I   T, or C-T-H-S-I-R

a vital message of greater significance than the mere recognition of His name: Christ the Holy Savior Is Risen.

○ *Letters viewed on light board simultaneously:*
NEVER

Sentence on light board:
THE RESULT OF NEVER IS EVER WITH THE END AT THE BEGINNING.

○ *Letters upon the light board:*
ANOTHER ENDING

The storyteller, still suspended, begins again.

What is the tongue of the tide, the bound, the rapt? Cleopatra is washed, dropped into a tub of turpentine, dried in the sun upon a bed of leech. An emollient of Ganges mud and locust sap is injected into her withered circulation system before she is rolled into a package of eucalyptus leaves locked with wax. Then the papyrus, strip after strip is wound round the torso. It takes all day. The legs are tethered. In the moonlight they turban her head. This is repeated and repeated and repeated and repeated. Now it is night again. At the break of day, nonetheless, the slaves say in their sleep they heard her talk.

On a projected slide a woman sits on a porch with a cat curled into her lap.

○ *Letters upon the light board:*
MARMALADE

The man recalls another strange event.

One morning our maid—a black woman imported from the States, who (I perceive in

26

retrospect) in rhyming homonyms corrected for dyslexia—asked my mother if she wanted some "carmelmade." My mother, a quiet and refined woman, thought about it for a second or so before she burst out in a laugh that I could not believe came from her throat. My sister and I stared at one another in shared disbelief, and our eyes soon again met in fright and then in terror as my mother lingered in her laugh. We rose from the table but she persevered; we sat again, but yet no stop.

The maid, Doris, looked on in confusion for a minute or more. And then she did something more horrible, to our way of thinking then, than we had ever witnessed. Bending down, as low almost as the breakfast plates, she put her head at the level of my mother's and commanded her to stop; and when the howling did not cease, she took her hand up and swung it through the air to land upon my mother as a slap.

We couldn't be certain now whether mother was laughing still or whimpering. "Go call your daddy!" this virago hissed.

My father later told us, it was a fit. But we could not determine whether he was speaking of the maid or of our mother.

The maid left a few days hence, not, I now suspect, because of her action—for we had told no one, and mother would not speak for weeks—but because of our silence in her presence. For she was a stranger now in the house where she had never needed to know French.

⊙ *Letters upon light board*:
THE MAN WHO HATES YOU

Sentence upon light board:
WILL GOOD SOCIETY NEVER LEARN THAT OFTEN IT IS BEST TO KEEP THE MAN WHO HATES YOU MOST IN YOUR BED?

○ *Letters upon light board*:
THE VICTIM

The journalist again reports.

Very clever, very clever, spoke Reason, to lie down with the man you shoot and arise his prey. Like a phoenix who first sets the pyre afire and then lying upon it cries out it's killing me! The pain! Everyone from miles around gathers to applaud the transformation. A miracle!—
  Of sorts. But in your mouth I found a feather!
  What do you mean? asked the victim from his hospital bed.
  You're alive. He is dead.
  Yes?
  He has buried his body in your head. I'll be listening for the rattle.

○ *Letters upon the light board*:
SALUT

The suspended storyteller tries again.

There is Georges and Claude and Louis and Robert—all my uncles and aunts at table together! It is a feast! proclaims my father, for the eyes as well as for the gut! For *gut* as well as the belly adds Louis, who married an Alsatian. For family ties and *Gott,* laughs Georges, who recently was ordained a priest. Robert, rotund from birth totters to his feet: For the thread that binds and the belt we'll soon let loose! All faces turn toward Claude, who grins. When he finally speaks it is in a whisper instead of a shout. To morrow's sighs: for gotten paunch!
  Talks like a fortune cookie says my aunt Monette. Are we going to swallow platitudes or meat?

◗ *Letters upon the light board*:
ALLER ET RETOUR

The poet cannot resist.

There was a woman from where she was who went out the door to before and came in again to then. And there she sat once more leaving what was left to after her action. Down on his luck her husband got up to cross himself and room already to where he was about to be not anymore. She, stayed, wasn't about to be moved this time come well or ill until taken.

On homemade film a woman stands upon a mountain, enters an adobe, greets an Indian with an open palm as in movies.

◗ *Letters upon the light board*:
THE PICKLE

Once again, the storyteller

I do not like pickles! Yet time and again he puts a pickle on my plate! I do not like it!
He giggles.
Oh, I forgot.
I don't like it on my meat or my bread!
He takes away the pickle and brings back the plate.
You do this on purpose!
You don't relish my little gherkin?
Every time I tell you I don't like the taste.
Don't tease him, Pierre. It's only a cucumber, dear, washed in a little vinegar bath.
It tastes sour.

This one was sweet.

I'm getting angry because we've been over all of that. Don't ever serve me a pickle again!

Pierre clucks.

Since he doesn't want a pickle, Pierre, why do you torture him?

I'm not torturing the boy, but you're clearly spoiling the brat. When we're gone and dead and he gets served a pickle, is he going to throw a fit?

I suppose he will tell them—the waiters and such—not to serve him it.

And what if they forget, is he going to carry on and shout?

I'll tell them to take the plate back and serve me again the way I asked.

What if he's having lunch with his boss and with the pâté the wife serves cornichons? How long do you suppose he'll last?

I won't work for a man who presumes his employees eat pickles for lunch.

It's not the eating that matters, but your reaction to the expectation you might. Marie doesn't like jam, but when served it she doesn't fuss. She eats instead the things she prefers and puts the jam back into the pot.

I don't like pickles either.

He's always putting one on or beside my baguette. I don't even want it to touch!

They put jam on my croissant.

So we do, dear. And that is, I believe, precisely Pierre's point. You're not always going to get things the way you do here. And there's no use complaining. It will get you into trouble, and there will be no one there to help out.

But I've never been in trouble. Can they arrest a man who doesn't like pickles or jam?

I should think not. But you understand, dear, don't you, when I say adolescents often arrest their own growth from childhood to their position in society as responsible adults?

If I promise not to make a fuss, will you promise to try to remember to never put a pickle on my plate again?

No, I can't.
Pierre!
Then someday, I guess, I'm going to get into a pinch.

The dumbshow simultaneously represents a tableau of uncles, aunts, good food, and toasts.

◉ *Letters upon the light board:*
THE WAKE

The woman on the mountain speaks like a girl of then.

When at the wake of Aunt Monette my mother let a gutsy laugh slip from her lungs out through lips, everyone was afraid, less for its consequence—the inevitable return to "sanitorium" (their euphemism for the mental ward of our provincial prison)—than for its continuance. But my mother, immediately silencing herself, shocked them even more by what she said: I can't comprehend why everyone is always smiling at the newborn and crying for the dead. That such complete release from the suffering and consternation trapped through a lifetime in the human head should not be a cause to roar with absolute relief to me makes no sense. On the other hand, a baby's birth, bringing with it the certainty that this new human will be subject to all the punishment and pain produced by her stay on this earth, overwhelms me in waves of nausea and despair.

Indeed, in reaction to the thought tears freely fell. And so the aunts, after comforting her with pats upon shoulders, head and back, were appeased and beginning in again to chat, reminisced about this and that which brought forth occasionally a chuckle and even once or twice a little laugh.

● *Letters upon the light board*:
MEMORIZATION

The man recalls what he cannot.

Right in the middle of forgetting I forgot, remembering at last what was about to be lost. Yet it had apparently passed, since I could not now recall why I had wanted to forget or why in the midst of forgetting I could suddenly recall all. Eventually I knew I would forget and having forgotten would attempt to recall what I had this time not. Fearing that, I attempted to memorize the past, and repeating it over and over, in retrospect, I begin to realize that I had already forgotten a lot, the colors of clothes and rooms, the smells of—was it summer? the seasons, the sounds of certain voices, and the sources of the voices themselves. Now I knew everything only in outline, and the more I retraced the outline the more I comprehended how its contents had been condensed, until I saw what was within as only a spot, a dot that stood for all that it was and could then have been. Until it appeared that nothing really had occurred, although it might have if only I had drawn in a deeper breath or studied the ceiling, a dress, or listened for what must or should have been said. And so it seemed now that nothing really had been spoken—although there were certain sentences that I seemed to remember such as: Are you certain? And as certain in such a circumstance as such an uncertain person as me can be—or accomplished by my committing it to memory, or even remembered and finally forgot.

● *Letters upon the light board*:
REMEMBERING AND FORGETTING

Sentence upon the light board:
BETWEEN REMEMBERING AND FORGETTING IS THE DISTANCE OF THE BEARER AND HIS BURDEN.

◑ *Letters upon the light board*:
CAUSE AND EFFECT

Back to the suspense

Staring into Rue Cassette Raison saw a patch—obviously not the kind one puts over one's eye but left by a tire of a taxi perhaps. He took a monocle from and put it immediately back into the pocket of his black double-breasted blazer. His eyes watering in the sun, he sought a café where he might sit out the rest of the day. Yawning, he found a canopied seat into which he collapsed to order cassis.

On film a detective sits upon a park bench, opens a book, and notices the details of the trees, visitors' attitudes and dress.

◑ *Letters upon the light board*:
PASSOVER

In center stage, Mr. Croset

At the table a man began the tea time ritual. I saw immediately how similar it was to the mass, and took into my hands the Torah, where I read: As the sand is between the toes so shall they become a bower to the sun. Surprised to see such words upon those pages, I closed my eyes in a complete acceptance of death. When nothing happened, I opened them again and, with an Irish accent, said: I have worked hard to die. Since the angel has passed me by it's my turn to pay for your pints!

● *Letters upon the light board:*
FLAT

Suspended storyteller describes an upcoming event.

On the left is a house, a wall with ivy pulled from it. The fence has fallen. A tree stands out from behind, giving the flat surface. And so it is the way the British describe compartments. You do not knock. A bell does not function. A key is required. For example there is no plant in a pot. Generally not. No one to run to. Although there may or may not be a man with a hat. Certainly he will ask why you have come. But often there is no one. And you must leave to come back.

● *Letters upon the light board:*
RELIEF

The woman with the open palm recounts.

My first father was fat. Poulet en Cocotte Bonne Femme, Caneton Rôti à l'Alsaciennce, Tournedos Rossini, Carbonnades à la Flammande, Farce aux Rognons, Gigot ou Épaule de Pré-Salé Braisé aux Haricots, Blanquette de Veau à l'Ancienne, Fricadelles de Veau Duxelles, Rôti de Porc aux Novets, Jambon Farci en Croûte, Cassoulet de Porc et de Mouton, Foie de Veau à la Moutarde, Ris de Veau Braisés à l'Italienne, and Cervelles en Matelot were a few of his favorites. After his Black Peach Brandy with a pit perched at the bottom of the bottle, he would sit back and unbutton the top of his trousers. Exhaling, he told us daily this was the moment for which he lived.

Look around you and remember everything you see. Don't forget that chair over there, that bit of fluff the maid forgot to sweep up. And watching my mother bend to carry it off, he propelled the air from his jowls with a sound that consolidated his relief with his exasperation. And most of all you must always recall everything your mother attempts to wipe out of sight. The world is a body, just like me, grossly overweight and impolite. Come, snuggle up to it for a bit.

A film simultaneously depicts a boy, trapped. He is kissed and doesn't mind it.

◐ *Letters upon the light board:*
SEEING AND BELIEVING

Sentence upon the light board:
BETWEEN SEEING AND BELIEVING IS THE DISTANCE OF THE EYES TO THE BRAIN.

Total blackout.
In the darkness one hears knocks.

◐ *Letters upon the light board:*
THE FRIEND

THE STORYTELLER: Raison knocks. Knocks. Knocks once more. But no one comes for him. He takes a tie pin from his pocket and puts it in the lock, playing with the tumbler until he feels it give. As suddenly the door falls open from within, and his eyes meet a belly, not bulging, but tight, trim.
  Two figures appear on opposite sides of a slightly opened door.
THE MAN WHO RECALLS: Monsieur?
THE DETECTIVE: No one answered.
THE MAN WHO RECALLS: No one ever does.

Simultaneously a series of slides depict a flat, from its exterior, its lobby, odd angles, windows, segueing into a room where a man sits naked on the edge of the bed.

THE DETECTIVE: Monsieur Croset, I presume.

THE MAN WHO RECALLS: I am a friend.

THE DETECTIVE: Ah.

THE MAN WHO RECALLS: I am going out.

THE DETECTIVE: May I come in?

THE MAN WHO RECALLS: Perhaps you should ask Madame about that?

THE DETECTIVE: But as I reported, no one came for me before.

THE MAN WHO RECALLS: You could phone.

THE DETECTIVE: I had an appointment.

THE MAN WHO RECALLS: Ah.

THE DETECTIVE: So, may I come in?

THE MAN WHO RECALLS: Perhaps you should wait until I come back.

THE DETECTIVE: Now see here!

THE MAN WHO RECALLS: Are you a burglar?

THE DETECTIVE: Quite the opposite.

THE MAN WHO RECALLS: A copper?

THE DETECTIVE: A policeman.

THE MAN WHO RECALLS: Well that explains it then.

THE DETECTIVE: Explains what?

THE MAN WHO RECALLS: Why you fiddled with the lock.

THE DETECTIVE: No one answered.

THE MAN WHO RECALLS: No one's there.

THE DETECTIVE: But you—you were within.

THE MAN WHO RECALLS: But as you see, I am about to be out, and would have been if you had not stood in the door.

THE DETECTIVE: Come now, let us get this settled.

THE MAN WHO RECALLS: Where do you propose to take me?

THE DETECTIVE: Pardon?

THE MAN WHO RECALLS: And come to think of it, why should I join you? I have my own business to attend. Unless, of course, I am under arrest?

THE DETECTIVE: Monsieur, I am not proposing you physically accompany me. I meant simply for you to join me mentally in trying to deduce whether or not Monsieur or Madame are in their house.

THE MAN WHO RECALLS: Well, you may join me if you want. But I am not certain as to where I am headed.

THE DETECTIVE: I do not want to go out. I want to get in!

THE MAN WHO RECALLS: That's what they all say.

THE DETECTIVE: Who?

THE MAN WHO RECALLS: The riff-raff. That's why people have locks.

THE DETECTIVE: But I was invited for a friendly chat.

THE MAN WHO RECALLS: Too late! We have already had one. I remind you, I am their friend. As you might also have been had you strolled with me round the Tuileries.

THE DETECTIVE: Let me try again. Do you know where Monsieur and Madame might have gone?

THE MAN WHO RECALLS: Practically anywhere.

THE DETECTIVE: Do you know where they are likely to have gone?

THE MAN WHO RECALLS: Out of course!

THE DETECTIVE: For how long?

THE MAN WHO RECALLS: Oh, maybe a minute or two…

THE DETECTIVE: Might I wait in the living room for their return?

THE MAN WHO RECALLS: Or, maybe a month.

THE DETECTIVE: You are exasperating me.

THE MAN WHO RECALLS: As you are delaying me. Am I or am I not under arrest?

THE DETECTIVE: I do not appear here in my capacity of detective.

THE MAN WHO RECALLS: You said you were a copper.

THE DETECTIVE: I am a policeman, in the general sense. But I am not visiting on that account.

THE MAN WHO RECALLS: Ah. But then why have you come? If you are not really a copper or even a dick? Are you a bum?

*The series of slide pro-
jections is repeated.*

THE DETECTIVE: Pardon?

THE MAN WHO RECALLS: A landlord? A fire inspector? An artist?

THE DETECTIVE: No. No. No. None of those.

THE MAN WHO RECALLS: A murderer then?

THE DETECTIVE: I am pondering it.

THE MAN WHO RECALLS: That is what I have been saying. People have to have locks. Sometimes it is important to keep people out.

THE DETECTIVE: Then why have they let you in?

THE MAN WHO RECALLS: Perhaps it was I who let in them?

THE DETECTIVE: Monsieur, I am beginning to suspect that you are not, so to speak, "all there."

THE MAN WHO RECALLS: Perhaps you are correct. Am I a figment of your conscience?

THE DETECTIVE: I have nothing to feel guilty about!

THE MAN WHO RECALLS: Then, I'm off!

THE DETECTIVE: Let me begin at the beginning. Please, go back inside. I shall come up the walk and knock. You shall answer the door and say "Hello, may I help you." And I shall say, "Yes, I am here to speak with the Crosets. They have invited me to lunch." And you shall say "Come in. I'll fetch Monsieur and Madame." And I shall enter the parlour where the maid shall take my coat and hat.

THE MAN WHO RECALLS: What shall she do with them?

THE DETECTIVE: It doesn't matter!

THE MAN WHO RECALLS: Oh, but you see, it does. How can we play the go-betweens of intrusion and domesticity if all is as vague as that? The maid must know what to do with the props.

THE DETECTIVE: I am not an intruder, and I doubt the Crosets might ever have represented domestic tranquillity to anyone.

THE MAN WHO RECALLS: Are you suggesting they are not a happy couple, blessed to be living at this lovely bougainvillaea-covered house on Rue Casette?

THE DETECTIVE: I do not know them yet.

38

THE MAN WHO RECALLS: Then why are you accusing them?

THE DETECTIVE: I accuse them of nothing. …But there are rumors. And the Crosets, each of whom—one hears—has lovers, do not appear to be a perfect match.

THE MAN WHO RECALLS: Ah. Rumors.

THE DETECTIVE: Well, if you must know, I have seen Mr. Croset in the company of his friend.

THE MAN WHO RECALLS: Friend? May I remind you….

THE DETECTIVE: Lover.

THE MAN WHO RECALLS: Ah. How tall?

THE DETECTIVE: About as tall as you.

THE MAN WHO RECALLS: Hair?

THE DETECTIVE: What is this? A cross-examination? I do not know everything.

THE MAN WHO RECALLS: But, gradually things are beginning to take shape. Although your scenario, I must admit, is a little predictable.

THE DETECTIVE: Blond.

THE MAN WHO RECALLS: Ah. Dress?

THE DETECTIVE: No.

THE MAN WHO RECALLS: No?

THE DETECTIVE: Pants.

THE MAN WHO RECALLS: Oh. What color?

THE DETECTIVE: Black.

THE MAN WHO RECALLS: Like these?

THE DETECTIVE: Yes, only pleated.

THE MAN WHO RECALLS: Such a careful observer—and you say you don't know everything! I bet you know exactly what she looked like.

THE DETECTIVE: It wasn't a she.

THE MAN WHO RECALLS: Ah. And how did you know they were more than just friends?

THE DETECTIVE: I saw them…they did more than talk.

THE MAN WHO RECALLS: You saw them through windows perhaps?

THE DETECTIVE: Through binoculars.

THE MAN WHO RECALLS: So you are a spy then?

THE DETECTIVE: I am a detective, as I said.

THE MAN WHO RECALLS: And what else did you detect? Did this lover love Monsieur Croset? Would he protect him from losing even his wife? Would he stand in a door to keep truth out?

THE DETECTIVE: Ah. Yes, I suspect he might.

THE MAN WHO RECALLS: The maid hangs the coat in the hall closet perhaps?

THE DETECTIVE: Where are the Crosets?

THE MAN WHO RECALLS: And on a chair beside the door she places the hat. She goes upstairs to tell them what perhaps I would not, that in the parlour waits a would-be friend, a copper who has come, so he says, not about his business.

THE DETECTIVE: Let me pass!

THE MAN WHO RECALLS: But you have failed every test. Liar, accuser, voyeur, burglar, murderer—at least in thought. You are why we shutter our windows and close our doors. …And I am why people still walk the streets each night.

THE DETECTIVE: In the name of the law, you are under arrest.

THE MAN WHO RECALLS: Come in. Come in.

◗ *Letters upon the light board*:
UNDER ARREST

The poet laments.

One speaks or speaks not or says or says not whether or whatever for what? For the afternoon or to hesitate perhaps hearing oneself say nothing into eternity? What does or doesn't silence one speaks for itself: the cicadas click in their sleep. And still you speak only in thought.

In center stage a man is revealed with bright white light, buried in the sand. He silently lectures to the stones and shells littered about.

◗ *Letters upon the light board:*
THE CONVERSATION

The man dreams his memories.

In my sleep a woman handed me a baby and asked if the mother were near to nurse. I said yes, but remembering then I had no wife, admitted she was not.

Then hold the baby tight!

I lifted it up against my chest. The child began to suck my ear and babbled into it. The women smiled in their seats across from me where they sat.

Soon I could comprehend everything the child said. And what first appeared as babble could be understood as coherent thought. The child asked me, What do you like best?

I like to travel, I answered, surprised at the response.

Travel isn't everything, spoke the child.

Oh, I know that! I agreed. And the women stared at me disapprovingly, as if I had been talking to myself. For, I suddenly understand, they heard the child's words as nothing but babble. To them, nothing made sense.

Here, let me take the baby, the aggressive one suggested. But I held the baby close in conversation, until they called the porter and demanded the child be returned to them.

◉ *Letters upon the light board*:
MUNDANITY

Sentence upon the light board:
It is always the mundane that reveals the insane history.

Complete blackout

TWELVE TYRANTS BETWEEN ACTS; or,
MUNDANE MOMENTS AND INSANE HISTORIES

Out of darkness the light board flashes:
IT IS ALWAYS THE MUNDANE THAT REVEALS THE INSANE HISTORY.

A performer, heavily made-up and dressed in the costume of a vaudevillian comic, finds his way through the curtain part.

Good evening Hades and Recompense. Lovely to be, hear the one about Mussolini?

Delivers the "Twelve Shticks" in the style of a stand-up comedian

❍ *A woman with little on puts a placard upon a stand:*
MUSSOLINI SHTICK

Mussolini was on the soap. His face promoted perfume. His fists clenched in anticipation for a chocolate. Bare-breasted, his likeness was attached to swimming trunks. A man paid a fortune for a chair in which Mussolini was said to have sat. Scraps of his hair went to museums. A church in Fabriano encased his spaghetti fork in glass.
    "To what do you attribute your immense popularity?" an unwary journalist asked.
    "I am the populace!" Il Duce screamed back.

43

"Well, then, how come you to be such a favorite of yourself?"
"You may put away your pen. You won't be needing it again!"

A rim shot and cymbal crash

● *The woman puts a placard upon the stand:*
THE DOWAGER EMPRESS SHTICK

When escorted into the room, and her eyes have become adjusted to the dark, the artist sees the Dowager seated upon a teakwood throne, circular in shape, carved with birds and Buddhas and fruits. Her Highness holds in the palm of her hand a lotus into which, as the artist goes forward, she plunges her nose as if to suck in the essence of it.

The artist raises the hem of her dress ever so slightly and bends, imperceptibly almost, from the neck. The Empress does indeed appear to be an empress in the manner one, at least an American, filled with fables and disgust of such potentates, might expect. Yet the Empress Dowager, she reminds herself, has been kind to the visitor during these first months. Two eunuchs behind Her Highness hum an inharmonious hymn. Everything is pleasant.

Suddenly dogs, three Pekingese pugs and a sort of Skye terrier, splutter across the rice-mat floor and fall in pants at Her Highness' feet. Their heads are patted. The artist delightedly taps the floor, but the pugs pay her no respect. Only the terrier advances shyly toward the hand held first palm out and then turned gradually in to pet. The dog accepts.

In an instant, the artist looks back to the recalcitrant ones, who hover still beneath the green nail sheaths. The artist smiles, following the curves of the finger and hand with her eyes up the arm of the Empress to witness a face flushed, furious, the flower hurled to the floor in apparent disgust. The hand of the artist instinctively pulls back from the beast, who growls in fear of its sudden jerk. Now the Empress is smiling again.

Rim shot, drum roll and gong

❿ *The woman puts a placard on the stand*:
FRANCO SHTICK

On the wall, backed by a tapestry in black, hangs an ivory crucifix, training all attention to the desk on which, in utterly ordered stacks, sit piles and piles of papers. In the center the Caudillo sits, writing a scenario for motion pictures.

> The camera pans the room. Focuses on desk.
> A hand. Hits the inkpot, spills. It is blood.
> Camera zooms back. Victim lies dead, head across
> the blotter, hand outstretched.

> Enter the detective.

> His pulse is checked.

Drum role, cymbal, a couple of machine-gun blasts

❿ *The woman puts a placard on the stand*:
DIONYSIUS SHTICK

My mother and I sometimes were invited to share the company of Dionysius. The guards brought us always into an outer chamber where they stripped away our clothing. One held me close; another my mother, fondling us in the excuses of a search. Might we not hide within our folds destructive weapons?

When our bodies had been thoroughly looked into, we were awarded white robes and entry into his presence.

He kept us at a distance, terrified that some secret missile might have been missed. He spoke little, for he feared that anything he told us might be useful in a plot.

And so was my mother hidden from all others, and I from anyone save tongueless nurses and toadying servants. Except for gold trinkets, heaping platters of lamb and apricots, and the pleasurable sensations of the male and female paramours pulling at my penis and licking my navel free of sweat, I knew nothing of the world. Like a pet, I was simply "kept"; kept as if all that really mattered lay in the territory bound between my eyes and my ass.

The Academy taught me that I also had a mind and feet upon which to stand it.

A dagger plunge, escape of breath and body drop

◗ *The woman puts a placard on the stand:*
NERO SHTICK

In Rome, I attended the phyrric performance of the flight of Icarus. Never before have I seen such a glorious event. It began in the dark of Dædaelus' labyrinth, the audience straining to spot the artist at his work. Upon the entry of the son, however, the walls came alive with the lights of more than fifty flaming torches lit all at once, so that they burnt momentarily into our sight. And when we had recovered our vision, we witnessed that the walls were trimmed in amber and amethyst. Rubies hung in ropes as emblems of stalactites against the cave's lustrous walls, where emeralds represented moss.

Now we could recognize the alchemist's art. As the son danced out the message of their necessary flight, the father unfolded a set of wings, white as marble, that spread a full twenty hands. And in a ritual dance, with some sexual gestures, he fit the contraption upon the boy's back.

When his son had returned the favor, he and Icarus rose through the flambeaus into a gold-studded sky of stars and flew off into dark.

Suddenly the black was illuminated from below, at first faintly, but in a suspenseful pace, gradually growing lighter and lighter until it reached the floor over which the heroes were suspended. The sun was a ring of fire, through which, when it had approached its proper height, the father flew expertly. But the son, as in the old stories, was singed by the flames, and unable to keep his balance upon the wires to which he was attached, fell to the bottom too fast. Blood splattered upon Nero himself, who sat in a seat overhanging the stage's apron.

At first the audience could not determine whether or not what had happened was part of the plot. And when a cry arose from the chorus, there was near pandemonium. But the emperor appeared to be nonchalant as he took a bit of the blood upon a finger and licked it off. And so the crowd was calmed.

A round of applause and burst of dynamite

● *The woman puts a placard on the stand*:
JOHANNITZA SHTICK

Johannitza, King of all Wallachia and Bulgaria, was irritated with his son who sat with colored cloth crying because he could not cut. The scissors lay at his feet before him.

The King tossed the remaining boot which his equerry had been attempting to remove over the head of his suddenly terrified son, who cried now more out of fear than out of frustration.

"You! It's simple!" And taking scissors to cloth he cut into it deep. "Cut and release cut release cut release cut…"

The cloth, witness to his acts, was in threads, which he as suddenly thrust with the scissors at the boy, running from the room in disgust.

The child, observing his own blood, was so fascinated with it, he shut up.

Guillotine slam and scream

○ *The woman puts a placard on the stand*:
KISSINGER SHTICK

Dr. Kissinger was most disturbed in Hanoi, detached, even dejected. The Paris Accords were all quite meaningless, given the North Vietnamese distrust of the West. Trying their best, they put him in a large suite. But despite the forest of lights, despite the enormous size of the room, atypical in Asia, he was sceptical yet. Each light, for example, had a different switch, so that when it came time for bed he had to scramble about the place, half undressed, to turn the lights out one by one. And when, in pitch-black, he finished and was ready to return, a host of mosquitoes followed him through the netting, so difficult to negotiate in complete darkness, into the bed. His sleep was fitful. And in the morning he could only wonder was it an accident that the masses gathered beneath his window for calisthenics at five-thirty AM?

A drum roll, flourish of trumpet

○ *The woman puts a placard on the stand*:
HALAGU SHTICK

It was Halagu, as we have heard, who tricked the Caliph of Baghdad by charging with a mere column of men toward the wall of the great city.

The Caliph laughed when he saw these rag-tag troops and took a handful of

Mohammedans down to destroy them. The band took flight and, trailed to the edge of a woods, suddenly turned on their stalkers as a battalion appeared from east of the forest and another from the west, who together with the band of original men surrounded and captured the Caliph and his forces.

So the Tartars rode into that city of such wealth that legends of its golden streets are still quoted in some sources.

But there were no golden streets. There was poverty instead. There were many beggars. The palace was impressive, but pearls compare poorly with what the imagination has wrought.

Halagu, pleased with himself, sent messengers to his conqueror brothers in the north, the east, the west. But he was disappointed nonetheless. As he sat upon the throne of the Caliph he wondered, momentarily of course, why he had chosen to rule the southern section of the universe. But there is a breeze in that valley at night that blows through the palms and rustles the silk of the blouse. And so he stood with the moon to his face and back to minaret.

Sword upon sword, metal against metal

○ *The woman puts a placard on the stand*:
BORGIA SHTICK

Fellow ladies: Dress may henceforth be of worth no more than 50 ducats, to be furnished with gems, stones, and glass equal to. China silk shall not be worn in public, nor velvet, embroidered damask, nor satin. Lace from the Spanish, applied to sleeves and hem, may not be attached to bodice. Gems such as silver and gold may be implanted upon the dress unless assessed at more than 50 ducats, but emeralds, rubies, sapphires, jade, black pearls and diamonds may not be put on anywhere. Fourteen clasps may be attached to the back, two at the frontice. Sleeves shall not be more than three hands of your daughters deep, flounce and ruffle no more than ten.

Shall these rules be neglected I have put in the cathedral and every church boxes into which fathers, husbands, lovers, and those women prim and properly attired may drop a complaint of size, sleeve, or superciliousness of style.

LUCREZIA, DUCHESS OF FERRARA

Reports of a firing squad

❍ *The woman puts a placard on the stand:*
STALIN SHTICK

The gardens at Gagra are glorious on summer nights. Above the Tsikherva is a villa where, when the sun lies low upon the canyon, roses light up in ochres and reds. "The air here," the visitor, the Gensek himself, observed "is almost too sweet to suck up one's nose." Everyone agrees.

Koba, the Father of the Peoples, is taken down another path and another where fuschia and iris are planted in patterns punctuated with imported peonies. "For me," muses the Great Master of Abrupt Turns and Revolutionary Daring, "it is too pleasant to pass another moment in this place." And with that he marches his party about face and out through the gate.

His host apologizes for the humidity that hangs upon the river bank. "But why, Joseph Vissarionovich, in such heat do you wear your boots yet?"

"How can I tell you of the comfort I find in them. Such a snug fit satisfies me as when a child is snuggled to his mother's teat. I am totally secure with them upon my feet, for if any one gets out of line you can kick him in the head so hard his mouth and his stomach shall never meet again.

The drone of a squadron of planes

50

◗ *The woman puts a placard on the stand*:
MOCTEZUMA SHTICK

He, Moctezuma, was a clean man who bathed daily twice. Dark, as the Indians are generally, he had no stubble upon his chin. He was tall and lean. He walked with great pride, upright in manner that led me to believe he was within what he appeared to my eyes. But wherever he went no one of his men might raise his gaze in that direction, so they could not see as we how a civilized man might look.

His court was richly dressed, each man in beads of shrimp and headgear of green and yellow feathers. Their pottery was as solid as that in Madrid. They sat at supper, he and six or eight others, at a table served by twenty of his wives for that reason selected. There were surrounding him jesters and cripples, dwarfs and jugglers, and further from the central porch, at least three thousand more who ate, after he, of the food remaining. They never again used the same pots.

He ate a wide assortment of meats, fowl, fish, maize, and grains not grown in our imaginations. Green fruits and bright red balls of substances at once gummy and sweet. Some have said he cooked and ate babies. But I have seen none, save, on occasion, the flesh of sacrificed fully grown women and men.

Sharp whistle, direct hit of bomb

◗ *The woman puts a placard on the stand*:
HITLER SHTICK

Blondi was the only one who aroused him to human feelings. The dog was obedient, carefully taught. At supper she sat a full two feet from her master, but gradually as it progressed so too did she, pulling by inches closer and closer until she had laid her head upon the Führer's feet. Sometimes he permitted her to stay.

But in the morning there were no alternatives. He greeted the dog with a flick of wrist which sent the beast upon the fetch. She was sent away again. And again. And again. Sometimes he permitted her to whimper and jump at the wire fence for a few attempts.

But then the dog was taken and put upon a piece of wood one foot wide by approximately twenty. And there, while he watched in joy, she balanced upon it above the ground at least six feet in the air.

The wood creaks with balance, back and forth, creaks.
Blackout
To the music of La Marseillaise the following information appears on the screen as in film credits:

The preceding fictions were based upon materials from the following sources:

Richard Collier. *Duce! A Biography of Benito Mussolini* (New York: Viking, 1971).

Katherine Augustus Carl. *With the Empress Dowager* (New York: Century, 1905).

S.F.A. Coles. *Franco of Spain* (London: Neville Spearman, 1955).

Plutarch. B. Perrin, trans., *Plutarch's Lives, VI: Dion and Brutus* (Cambridge, MA: Harvard University Press, 1918).

Miriam T. Griffin. *Nero: The End of A Dynasty* (New Haven: Yale University Press, 1984).

Geoffroy de Villehardouin. M.R.B. Shaw, trans., *The Conquest of Constantinople* (Harmondsworth, Middlesex, England: Penguin Books, 1963).

Henry Kissinger. *Years of Upheaval* (Boston: Little Brown, 1982).

Marco Polo. R.E. Latham, trans., *The Travels* (Harmondsworth, Middlesex, England: Penguin Books, 1958).

Anton Antonov-Ovseyenko. George Saunders, trans, *The Time of Stalin: Portrait of a Tyranny* (New York: Harper & Row, 1981).

Francisco Lopez de Gomara. Lesley Byrd Simpson, trans., *Cortés: The Life of the Conqueror* (Berkeley: University of California Press, 1964).

Albert Speer. Richard and Clara Winston, trans., *Inside the Third Reich* (New York: Macmillan, 1970)

○ *Letters appear upon the light board:*
GOOD AND BAD

The man remembers an important event

Now in Paris, one morning, the hands I seldom see touch me asleep, help me to sit upright, put me upon my feet, slipping over my nightshirt a pair of pants. They are pulling me, out, into the street, down another and some stairs, down into a cellar where we sit, sit forever it seems. Sometimes they cover my ears. But I hear things. Trucks. Somebody's slapping the street. I am afraid we will never leave.

After the hands slip from my ears I remember my sister and wonder where she and my father might be. My mother seems to be sorry, for suddenly she hugs me to her chest.

And after a while we come back to the night. As we ride up the lift, she bends to whisper into the right side of my head. "Now you shall stay indoors. I am sorry, but you can no longer play with your friends."

"Have I been bad?"

"No, my love, the world has been."

○ *Letters upon the light board:*
VOCABULARY

The storyteller, come down to earth

What do you have to say for yourself asked the man of the boy, who had never thought about saying anything for or about anyone, least of all himself.

I….

That's the start, the elder intervened, say it out!

You….

No, you have to take the responsibility for this.

What?

Come now, no innocent tricks.

The boy grew dumber yet.

Come on, I want the truth.

Truth was an even more shocking concept, one of those words used generally by adults to specifically describe their desires for the young.

I have to be honest.

That's what I expect.

I…he paused to see if perhaps the man might fill in the blank…don't know what you're talking about.

Why deny it, Claude? I've got evidence.

Evidence?

Unrefutable.

The child thought a while about the word just introduced. It sounded so permanent, like a dog barking at an open door towards which one had begun to walk upon locking the gate at back.

I'm waiting, threatened the adult.

So am I, spoke the child, shocked at the sound he had thrust into the space between the two of them.

So you admit it. And the punishment?

The child submitted, bowed head.

The guillotine!

In terror the boy surveyed the room for an escape.

But the hand reached round his waist. My little philistine!

The boy looked up in a last attempt to translate the tongue that was as suddenly inseparable from his.

On film or projected video a judge is discovered on the floor, dead. In his hand is a note. The detective enters, checks his pulse.

○ *Letters upon the light board:*
SERVICE

Chorus, alternating sentences

We give the tea and take the tea as time dictates, spooning out the Grey, Double Orient, and India Elixir, pleased if you may and just as happy if you're not. This is the cup, the saucer into which the spoon slid touches lips which go to say some things servants never. Repeat. And again today we place the platter upon the oak buffet, and over chatter splash the tea into every glass. We were saying what was certainly at tea never said for nothing enters any head-waiter's repartee. Come what may, we serve the tea, that is he or sometimes she, sniffing at the steam to see if enough has been put into the pot. If not we, he or she, go away and come back to here as if there was anything, in the fact that someone's seen and another's not, and another disappears in the setting. There is a mirror to turn into pretending to peer into sandwiches or little cakes or Sunday's kippers. And then when we, she or he, turn back they can better bow over what is now done. Nearly. Everything is taken off.

Then in the kitchen there are kisses and occasionally a zipper to come down with the little lemon tarts and hisses of the kettle in the servant's parts.

In a dumbshow, performed, stage right, a man attempts to enter a flat. He is met at the door by a maid who takes his coat and hat.

○ *Letters upon the light board*:
WOMEN AND MEN

The man who remembers is a boy again.

Stand up she said. And I did, to know who she was, who she thought, at least, I was or she to so command me. Come. And I just followed—into a room where I had never been, although I thought the house familiar. Her brother was my friend. And by force we had taken the parlour. The kitchen had been our line of last defense. As legionnaires we had ridden dromedaries through every bedroom but the one in which she hid. That, so Pierre proclaimed, was a den of secret spies. To enter would be automatically to die. So with stethoscopes we listened to the floor above it as we stood, barefoot by decree, upon the dining table. All she did was walk, but we interpreted the movement of her feet, nonetheless, as a sort of secret code that normally was listened to by servants, who passed their comprehension on to Belgians. Once she did a Spanish dance!

But now I didn't know where we were, she and I, in the dark inner sanctum of her father's study. It must have been the church, where, he once warned me, an old monk sat. I saw no one. But I knew he might come back and damn her on the spot where, on the very edge of the dark oak desk, she lifted the hem of her dress, by accident, it seemed, with a scratch of the ear, and then aware and startled by the act, dropped it back. But I had seen everything: her underwear was black.

My daddy doesn't live here anymore.

Why is that?

I think he got bored. You know my mother?

She's very nice.

Oh, she's an angel absolutely! But, you know, men sometimes want a woman to be a little naughty.

I don't. Why?

You know. They want a woman who, well, women who smoke and whisper in their ears and poke their ribs and blink their eyes about. I have heard several guests say my mother was blessed. But I have never heard her say anything in a voice that anyone couldn't hear or move her eyelids up or down or even wink. Everything she says is absolutely certain, spoken straight like she was looking right through the skin into your heart beating through the middle of your chest. I don't believe that appeals to men.

Does to me.

But you're just a boy. How could you comprehend?

I know a spy when I see one.

What spies? How?

They always try to get men into bed. And when they do, they sink their teeth into them. But you can always spot 'em—if you're clever. They never look you in the eyes. And generally they draw you into rooms in which you've never been. And then, ahead of time they show you what you're supposed to see later.

You sound so experienced.

And then they try to build you up. You know, encourage you to think how handsome you are and how you have such big muscles.

I bet you do.

And they're always touching arms and thighs and wherever else you might have developed one.

I thought guys like that.

Oh, they do! But, I don't like undercover agents. Cause as soon as you leave the room they tap out some secret to someone who you've never heard of and wouldn't even know if you met. Everything gets so confused. Who do you care about? The man in the moustache or the man who wears the hat? And for what does the man in the moustache or the man who wears the hat stand? Because maybe the handle-barred man likes only bare-headed men, and the man who wears the hat will shoot anyone who wears facial hair or who hasn't even shaved yet.

You're silly.

I know. But I'm correct.

Maybe you should have married my mother.

By the way, I admitted, I like your black negligee.

Silly boy, they're panties.

○ *Letters upon the light board*:
THE WELL

The gossip crossing the courtyard cannot resist another story.

Next Camelia comes…Ho! she is a sly one, she who blinks like a communion queen, all blushes for the bushes in which she's bent. And Dominique…a devil as well! She shall go straight to the water hole and lift her wonderful tale of woe while the bucket bumps to bottom and back. How the cad took her behind and again at the bend of the road and at crib with her keeping one in the cradle. And there were two, then three, and she said no before there were more. And off he strolled, wandered, slunk like a skunk into the arms of whoever it was, or would or could, girls, full-grown women, witches, boys in blue-jeans and even men. While she left to die with an entire trinity at teat, cried night and day until Camelia came to stay. Camelia is a saint. She can carry one off and put another upon her knee while the mother washes the re-

time to time, certain things such as I hope you have a nice day," "pretty thing," and "patience pays."

A mother is a mountain, immovable, marvelous and maddening at moments, sometimes days, even months. I knew a man once who had not spoken to his for thirty years, yet on weekly visits brought her presents, pears and purple plums. I should add, she never spoke to him since he'd run away with a man from Le Conquet, a town at the tip of it.

○ *Letters on light board*:
REUNION

A couple can be walking in the same or opposite directions, waiting on line for a taxi or in queue for bus.

HER: Guillaume? Guillaume?
HIM: Are you talking to me?
HER: Guillaume!
HIM: No.
HER: Now don't try to hide from me!
HIM: I'm sorry, Madame, but you've got the wrong man.
HER: Oh, I know. You probably think I'm propositioning you! But you needn't worry. I'm Patrice.
HIM: Thank you, Patrice, for alleviating my fears. Now…
HER: Everyone must try to start up a conversation with a handsome man like you.
HIM: No, fortunately not.
HER: You look almost as good today as then.
HIM: When?
HER: You know.
HIM: Ah, in the good old days, eh?

HER: They were, weren't they?

HIM: I wouldn't know.

HER: You never had a chance!

HIM: What do you mean?

HER: You tell me. A girl on every shoulder.

HIM: Oh. That popular, eh?

HER: Oh don't be so modest! I'm Patrice!

HIM: Evidently.

HER: Isn't it?

HIM: I'm sorry, Patrice….

HER: Oh, don't be sorry, I know I've changed radically. All puffy and fat. It's a wonder!

HIM: What?

HER: What?

HIM: What's a wonder?

HER: Well, a marvelous thing, of course!

HIM: Of course.

HER: To have run into you and have you recognize me after all these years.

HIM: How many?

HER: I'm not good at numbers.

HIM: Now who's being modest!

HER: I think it's called discreet. A woman can't be expected…

HIM: To recall such things.

HER: Oh, I recall everything!

HIM: I'm sure you do.

HER: Now you're being mean.

HIM: You needn't pout, Patrice, I don't remember much.

HER: Oh, in all honesty I've forgotten a lot.

HIM: And yet you expect me to recall something out of someone else's past?

HER: You're being uncooperative.

HIM: I mean, I'm not who you think I am.

HER: Is any of us?

HIM: I don't know who you are.

HER: How could you after the years like this. We have so much catching up.

HIM: It would help if I knew where to begin.

HER: You always were a strange mix.

HIM: Was I?

HER: That's what the girls used to say.

HIM: Did they?

HER: Yes. You kissed as sure and strong as Rock Hudson.

HIM: Really?

HER: And looked confused as Cary Grant.

HIM: Now there's a couple…

HER: Exactly. How could you miss?

HIM: That's what I've always wondered.

HER: You're mad at me, aren't you?

HIM: I'm not mad; amused, just amused I'd say.

HER: Yes, it always is.

HIM: What?

HER: So pleasant to see such a familiar face.

HIM: Yes. I should imagine.

HER: Well, you sure did.

HIM: Imagine?

HER: Remember the senior play?

HIM: I'm sorry….

HER: You should apologize!

HIM: For what?

HER: Teasing M. Boulanger like that!

HIM: I was a terror.

HER: Tell me.

HIM: No, I'd prefer you do the remembering.

A film represents a man standing with a cigarette in hand beside a bed. Another man enters and sits on the edge.

67

HER: I don't blame you....

HIM: I've forgotten everything.

HER: Tried to at least, I should guess.

HIM: As you'd have it.

HER: But you couldn't get her out of your head!

HIM: Her?

HER: Yes.

HIM: Perhaps.

HER: I mean, you loved her, didn't you?

HIM: Is that what everyone said?

HER: Goodness, no. Everyone said you couldn't care less.

HIM: Perhaps I did.

HER: No, you were careless, but you loved her. I could always see that.

HIM: And what about you?

HER: Me?

HIM: Married?

HER: Obviously.

HIM: Did I know him?

HER: No, you couldn't have. Albert Croset.

HIM: Albert Baptiste Croset?

HER: Yes!

HIM: I do know him!

HER: How could you. He's from Brest!

HIM: Well?

HER: And you, growing up in Lyon like that!

HIM: Oh.

HER: Well, I admit it. Villeurbane really.

HIM: That poor?

HER: A Jew!

HIM: Jewish. I've always wanted that.

In the film the man on the bed lifts his shirt, pulling it over his head. The smoker never reacts.

68

HER: Wanted what?

HIM: Family, tradition.

HER: Nobody else did. We were sick to death of our mothers, fathers, sisters, brothers. Remember the time I locked my sister in the attic and she called the cops?

HIM: No.

HER: Well, I'm sure your father would.

HIM: My father?

HER: He was the one, silly, who had to come over and jimmy the lock. Babette was so mad she socked the poor man in the eye just for being there when he opened up.

He laughs.

HER: Gee, it's good to talk.

HIM: How did you meet Croset?

HER: At a dance. Well, not really a dance. I wasn't supposed to be there, and wasn't actually. I was visiting a friend and she said, let's go down to the Hotel St. Claire and pretend. You know, that's what we girls sometimes did, walk round the lobby in our full-length frocks and drag on cigarettes. And we felt just like women whom we'd seen in movies and magazines. And then this man comes out of another room and seeing us says "Up here, you two! " And up we went, right into the middle of a party for his sister's wedding, where everyone was dancing, so I danced.

HIM: Right into his heart!

HER: Well, not right, a bit to the left, left over, I mean, as we were after everyone. And he was very drunk! He asked me, would I dance a foxtrot, and…

HIM: I get the drift.

HER: I trotted.

HIM: And still are!

HER: I guess. He doesn't dance much anymore.

HIM: With you, that is.

HER: Yes. Do you still see him?

HIM: Haven't since the university.

The man upon the bed in the film takes his shoes off.

69

HER: Isn't that strange?

HIM: Strange?

HER: That you knew him before I did. And I knew you and you could have told me....

HIM: I couldn't have told you anything.

HER: Warned me then.

HIM: Warned you?

HER: You know…

HIM: Yes, I can guess.

HER: I'm lucky though, everyone says.

HIM: For having such a house.

HER: Oh yes. And a family.

HIM: Children?

HER: No. I'm barren, or maybe he doesn't have the right count, but he won't take the test. His mother lives with us.

HIM: And his brother?

HER: You know him?

HIM: Yes. I've seen him often. We're…friends.

In the film the man upon the bed lies down flat.

HER: Georges?

HIM: Georges, yes.

HER: Imagine that!

HIM: What?

HER: You knew Georges too!

HIM: But I didn't know you.

HER: But, Guillaume, don't say that!

HIM: All right. I've said enough I guess.

HER: No! Don't leave now. Tell me.

HIM: What? Tell you what?

HER: Tell me....

HIM: I was going to say, let's let the old days slide away. Let's just say, what's gone is… and we…have just met.

70

HER: Okay, if that's the way you want to play. Hello, Mr. Guillaume Robert.

HIM: Ah!

HER: You seem pleased?

HIM: No, just a bit shocked. You see, my name is Robert Williams!

HER: Glad to meet you, sir. My name is Croset, Patrice. Now I want you to tell me what I should do.

HIM: What are you talking about?

HER: You said you loved me.

HIM: When?

HER: Then. I was her, the one to which I referred.

HIM: You? I was in love with you?

HER: I was the only girl you wouldn't kiss.

HIM: And you interpreted it…

HER: As a certain sign. I was special, I was not to be touched.

HIM: Weren't there others?

HER: Only the ugly ones. But I was considered quite pretty in those days.

HIM: I'm sure you were.

HER: You must remember that!

HIM: [*with resignation*] Yes.

HER: [*in tears suddenly*] You see! I was correct!

HIM: Yes, I guess….

HER: But you've got to tell me now.

HIM: What?

HER: What I should do.

HIM: Go home. Never speak to a stranger again.

HER: Yes, I suppose that is best. But, you have to know, I never have.

HIM: What?

HER: Spoken to a man I didn't know—except for him!

HIM: Really?

HER: Guillaume, you've got to believe me. I loved you so!

HIM: Yes. [*He hugs her to him.*] Yes. Well, you never know.

HER: You never do, do you. Here we are, years after the fact, meeting this way on the Champs Elysées!

HIM: I'm sorry, my dear, but we're in the United States.

○ *Letters upon the light board*:
THE DANCE

The boy becomes the man.

That was the time I discovered myself, so to speak, leg first. Then to the feet. For hours on end I stood flamingoing on one and then the other, perched eternally, or pretending to be, for quickly I uncovered my calf, and could as suddenly spin, my penis pointing out between. It felt funny when the air was rushed.

Then to my torso. Hands on hips, I sucked my stomach in, bent back and flung myself across the bed. Sometimes I let my fingers slide clear from my nipples straight down to my knees. The room, my room now, stood as a stage with the shutters released to reveal the rows and rows of theatre seats. I moved through this space, kicking a foot out from time to time, in a spin, a bow, a settle into squat. I didn't know what it was I did, only that it was a necessary act, and I, possessed, practiced and practiced until I could balance with a leg stuck straight out with my finger touching the roll of my socks.

"Shame on you, stark naked like that," my father laughed.

"Shhh," I warned him, "No one is allowed through the stage door entrance during the act."

○ *Letters upon the light board*:
OCCUPATION

The woman in the homemade movie

So I took to the streets. What streets, what I, what taken? I wander, know no one, nothing of the strange customs there. Do you bow when you meet? Smile? Or is that sign of sexual insinuation? On a curb I sit. But what if there is no curb in this culture, no halt to hold all the hostility in? If you don't like someone shoot. There is blood on every bed.

I called to a passerby why? I walk because you sit she shouted. Was I lazy in her mind or did she not have such a concept? A drunk drank nearby and put out his hand for money. A grocer piled potatoes into a pile and patiently waited. Passersby pointedly passed up the drunk and what he was drinking and paid instead for the substance from which it and presumably he had been made. Everything here appeared as normal as any normality might. But I remembered what my father always said: It was with a potato peeler in the Great War I fought the bloodiest battle of my life.

I asked a stranger—it could have been anyone—had there ever been in this land a woman or man who had never bled? He pointed at the whore who stood by the door of the loo as if guarding not the pronoun, for then she might have wandered near and about, but as if protecting those within from what occurs when the silent finger is laid across the mouth. She so the stranger winked is as innocent as anyone might be.

I asked the virgin what turns you on. Anything she said. And what do you want out of life? To have everyone salivate at the sight of me and stay yet as far away as a discarded wife. What pleasure can there be in such a strange distance? Have you never felt desire to touch? When I was a child my mother slapped my fingers a second before they would have scorched upon the stove top. Hot she scolded, the word she used also to answer my inquiry of what I should say when men asked to put their things about upon and in me.

So that is how you became a whore? What war, what you, what becomes?

A dumbshow of the aunts and uncles is projected on the screen at back.
Temporary blackout

◗ *Letters on the light board:*
SUDDENLY

The Man Who Recalls

Suddenly I found myself at the windowpane, as if it had severed before. I could remember yesterday night. I could remember the sun coming through the crack. But after that everything else was blank. I was simply at bay watching below a soldier pulling a woman into the doorway. But she stood her spot, signaling, it seemed, for the soldier instead to walk. He came after her as she led, laughing, both of them, as he pulled one way and she the other.

It was only as she turned her face into the light that I recognized her as my mother.

◗ *Letters upon the light board:*
STILL LIFE

The storyteller still in place

M. Raison sat frozen in his place. What did it mean? Not his current immobility, but the action that precipitated his position. What was being said? Not by the static meta-

74

phor of folded fingers but by the words over which they were placed. In the shadow of his hands, these lines hid:

Out of tips seeds turn into eternity. A shoot does. Green roots the mud. The pie rises, the pige coos in the breeze. These are realities. But if I shout there is no one there to listen, watch.

Slide of trees, one of which is scratched
Immediately everything turns black.

An old man (pedant and philosopher) stands buried in the sand. One can see his head alone which says:

From where does such a vision of evil emanate?

How do those genetic memory chips of ancient cultural taboo transform themselves into the images cast by our minds into space? Are such visages products of a sort of psychodrama performed by the imagination upon the nerves linking cornea to brain? A kind of mass hysterical hallucination triggered not by the shared values of one's peers but by some Neanderthals that sat at the mouth a prehistoric cave? How horrible must have been that ancient apparition to have etched itself not in memory only but in chromosome!

Seeking as always a history for what lies outside of it, I can comprehend evil only as a vision of our species before its capacity to fear and loathe what it would become. In order to come into consciousness humankind must have had to define itself against what (s)he imagined s(he) unconsciously had been, done. Had she, like the tyger, torn the throat of her territorial combatant? Had he too thumped chest, jumped upon the hinds of a passing member of his kind? At first it all must have seemed natural enough—until she saw perhaps another of her species leap upon the wholly mammoth, at water's edge he reflected on the bear behind him. Thing next to thing, being against being, awoke them to what they were not.

Over many a millennium (wo)man came to see theirself as a "not thing": I am not that—moon, snake, grass. I am no man, as Odysseus reveals himself to Cyclops. But the Greeks, as we know—just as the Egyptians and Hebrews before them—were tricksters who had already come to understand what they were not and sought to find out

77

what they were in relation to the moon, snake—recently the grass, swallowed by the ocean had become the hair of Poseidon's head, there to entangle the unwary traveller tacking his way back to love and death.

The gods above (con)fused themselves still, as ancients had, with horse, doe, dog, swan. A few mortals such as Acteon and Leda got a peek at that prehistoric past, and occasionally a shepherd sacrificed a sheep to the good old days, but in general the human beast became an elitist as soon as s(he) comprehended his/her position.

Noah was spared the Flood not because he was morally superior to other men, but because, as our first bibliographer, he achieved his God-given task to lasso and list all that he wasn't, the success of which made him a good "man."

The myth of the Flood, accordingly, can be seen as a history of the Expulsion from Paradise, to which the myth of Adam and Eve serves as emblem and act: There is the Eve who holds the tail of a python wound round the Adam delirious in its embrace. Uncoiling the serpent from about the man and pulling it out of the woman's grasp, Noah stuffs it into a box and carries it off to his craft. It rains a lot. A new creature is borne waving away from what s(he) was.

In short, evil isn't a condition, but is a position, a positing of one beside its brother. Around, away, on, above—these spiral about the dark unknown roots of being as surely as the ivy about the ivory columns of a mausoleum. Evil is "a relationship of our present to a time without presence that we carry with us like tits and cock."

Slow dim

78

● *Letters appear upon the light board*:
TRISTAN AND ISOLDE

The Man Who Recalls

During the Occupation we held our breaths, tiptoed to table, whispered about everyday events, were embarrassed even for the flush of the toilette. We were no longer a family, but "The French," as if we had lost our identifying voices and become instead the general whine of the mass. Why are you looking at me like that? Take your eyes away for instance and when you look back you will witness the fact that I am my sister and she is her brother. I am a rabbit, she ducks. Delusions. My mother is another. My father is a fat female in a printed address: 28 Rue de Faubourg Saint-Denis. "Come by late when my mate is in bed."

He kisses the hand who shoots what he has to obey, as if this way abeyance might come, on a pale white horse, to lay the night at his feat. I saw some men bend to the relief of my papa in the pretense that he was his wife.

● *Letters upon the light board*:
NORMANDY

The priest genuflects.

Even before evening before the moon became divisible by the night before the war even before then when everything was all right before when it wasn't once again before the morning light let everyone see what it had hid before they fell into sleep they were awakening from before and saw what the sea had put upon the shore.

○ *Letters upon the light board*:
HOOCHIEKOOCHIE

The journalist giggles and sings.

> All the girls in France
> want a little elegance
> in a rustic manse
> where they can loose pants
> and slip in a trance
> into bed with their aunts.

On film a young man dances a free-form ballet in rhythm to the chant.

○ *Letters upon the light board*:
PREPARATION

The woman standing on the mountain at back

It is a preparing always, a preparation, cooking and putting out the food upon plates, washing the pots, the spoons, the glasses, which once in a while can be dropped. It is a picking up of pieces, a simmering of stew, a baking of cakes. Someone is born and another is sick. The gravy is stirred until thick, the meat boiled is cut and positioned upon rice, or chopped and ladled over potatoes. Porkchops are fried and fish. The plates are stuck each to each. An uncle dies. The aunt always did enjoy eggs poached in dill paste. Wipe another pan dry. There is bread never to be touched until toasted just right. And there is always a birthday and a cake to be baked and another uncle ready to go to his grave. At church the organist faints.

There are rhubarb pies and gooseberry shortcakes, and whole afternoons of putting up peaches and nights of keeping a compress against a hot face. There is a breath that smells of the stable. And always there is milk to be squeezed out of the cow, the egg to be pulled away from the hen, the ham to be taken out of the sow, candy to be carried as a surprise in the purse. I can see that the little girl is going to get well again.

Someone has actually eaten his horse! The mayor has gone to bed in a fever.

There is corn to be popped and peas to be shelled and beans to be put in a pot where they sit so it seems for a week. We hear the organist's husband has had a heart attack. It is time to brew some apricot brandy.

My brother's first is killed in a crash. My mother is ancient. I am making peanut brittle tonight.

● *Letter upon the light board*:
DIANA

The storyteller suspended almost to the ceiling

First she went South, straight into the desert. She wanted to dry out she said, not meaning what it meant. She had only recently begun to sip a little gin with twice the tonic normally mixed in. No, she felt somehow dispirited, dampened almost by the so many memories that her head had kept. Why couldn't she like her sons and daughters always said they did, forget: names, places, certain trifling events. Birthdays, for example, were punctually observed with cute cards and sometimes checks—not just for family and friends, but for the mailman (postal carrier they now called him), for the organist at church, even the milkman who had retired along with delivery in

1958. The man at the lumberyard—but he was different, being sort of an old beau from before, before everything that had happened: husband, three beautiful boys, two girls, and another who appeared never to have determined her sex. Actually, of course, she was absolutely determined in her total aversion to men. But that was the way to family and friends her deviant sexuality had been expressed. It's because God had planned for a balance but her husband, against her pleas, so desired another male at the time of her birth. You get confused that way, in the womb, she once confessed to the pastor of the First Presbyterian Church. The minister was embarrassed by what she said, since she had never sat in his pews before; being Catholic perhaps she expected him to absolve her and genuflect. God works in strange ways, was the only words he could express. Sure does, she answered. And that reminds me, today is my birthday and not a card from any of them. You need a sabbatical, her priest advised soon after. There's St. Mary's upstate or St. Benedict's in the West. A good week would bring the blush back to the cheek. Say a rosary for me, father, for I'm going away. And I don't mean to one of your damn little retreats, where the old sit up till ten to play bingo and stay awake the rest of the night to pray. Maybe it's a good thing you're going, he thought to himself before kissing her cross, his personal sign of farewell and affection.

She saw a gila monster and a rattlesnake and wasn't scared a bit. She saw some Indians and bought a blanket which she didn't like. She sat in an adobe for half an hour. She bought postcards and wrote everyone notes such as Here I am can you believe? arrowing in on the deepest caverns of a canyon, mountaintops, or behind painted rocks. She liked arrows and bought some for an Indian totem shop.

As soon as her skin got dry and rough she got herself a bow and went North again.

On film a woman looks deeply into a well where she witnesses a boy eating pickles.

82

ON THE RUN

Needing to lose a little weight, I began to run. I was out of shape. And hardly had I made it round the corner when my heart severely pounded and my breath came in pants. But I was determined, and I continued, at a slightly saner pace, to go on to the next and the next intersection after that. It still hurt to breathe a bit, but my heart, momentarily at least, had fallen into pace with my feet, and my feet with my gasps. I played a game: every major landmark along my way became a goal which lost its significance the moment it was passed. That fence with the unpainted gate, the gate, the oak at the corner of the old Dessientes estate, the newspaper kiosk. These were places where I longed to be and as suddenly as I was there I couldn't care about in the least. The cathedral St. Anne was my greatest desire to reach; but when I touched the cornerstone on my rush past, it had no meaning. I was baptized in its nave! How could I care at this moment more about the loo down the street? It hurt horribly to breathe and I almost tripped on the rise of the concrete.

With that near collapse there was in my mood a sudden shift. Who was watching me? Such a stumbling, heaving, heavy-breathing beast must appear as a madman. A quick look over my shoulder revealed no one. That did not mean I was not being watched. Was that the echo of my feet? I was a spy, a wanted man. The army had taken the city—or worse—I was in possession of the news they were soon to move upon the state. Mightn't I tell the neighbors, call to them like the American Revere, as I passed? I darted quick into an alley. I ran out through another one, past the Circle de Colombe, and was chased in and out of a walking path from La Jolla down to Fairfax. My nose was bleeding, my heart about to pop, but I could not stop. I was afraid for my life. My head hurt, pounding with each step, a head, anybody's now, fell behind, back into black.

Temporary blackout
Lights come up in city square with entire chorus

◉ *Letters upon light board*:
DON JUAN

The gossip pauses in her promenade.

He took his time, his pulse patterning the action of his wrist, waiting again to begin before backing off, breaking silence, breath beating time to heart, hurrying ahead and having to be by stillness slowed, slowly down to the temporary stop. Take my breath away, someone once said, which sounded like death, which he desired, he would insist, standing at the back of anybody's bedroom, always aside the open bed as if, so fully suited, someone might sincerely contradict his pose by reclining and being naked both.

Several always came into the room at those parties, perhaps to see how the rest lives or lives rest at such speed and success. He wasn't impressed—by either intruders or hosts, as if it were his—bed, room, guest stumbling into such sanctity she or he generally said oh I didn't see anyone here, which he appeared to have not. Still several did not commit the expected spin; some stayed, even those who might have been, since he was one of those who held people in his sway, for whom many—most— fell as quickly as into a swoon, too soon in the lurch for a faint, a peak and perhaps, normal posture back, inquiring how's the water back here or you seem to have found a cozy spot. He took a smoke. Several sat on the unmade bed (did he or some suddenly summoned servant turn the covers back?) and, as if hat in hand, made ready for the entreaty: think I'm getting chilly or wonder if it's got a lump, while he weighted to the wall prepared to lean as if Rome had taken an eternity to collapse. And still he stood, stockstill. No one on the bed said why are you keeping me here in such an abased position, but something like that must have crossed the minds of every man or woman wound up in such a state. Who are you? some must have asked. And he, as always, must have let a long sigh slip from throat, which really would send shivers through the muscles and really would leave a lump in their throats. I said, I'm not waiting here forever, you know.

84

● *Letters upon the light board*:
SET, SETTLE, SIT

The poet gesticulates.

The surest sign of a signifier is its signifying fire when you might have said liar! You're just crying wolf when you meant cheetah—that fast from bark to being up the tree. When the chips are down you're with them hacking away at reality, where the real tree falls and along with your tongue the cat gets a head.

● *Letters upon the light board*:
ROUND

Sentence upon the light board:
IN A BOUT THE FALL'S WHAT TO FLOOR?

● *Letters upon the light board*:
UNCLE

Journalist with news of the weak

Put yourself in my pajamas, he said, by which he meant position, positioning me to the proper place. Imagine a man like me and forty-five suddenly a face a boy like you with a lip as long as a sailor's leg. He didn't believe every seaman stood taller really than every man on land, just in the head; and they were not standing actually in his imagination but, as I was now, lying flat. And he wasn't truly talking about those things on which they walked but that stood between the two—by which, so he expressed it, he was "wounded always in the best of his breasts." Give me a fist and first thing they got a ring round my nose, and everything goes, feet falling faster than the will collapse. He meant….

He spoke like that, poetically several said; out of his head insisted most. The boy was never asked. He was sent by his mother to live with his rich uncle, although even during the War he knew he wasn't really relative, and after, had few values left.

Why did she call you that?

What little elephant?

My uncle?

You ever played the game?

Of course! But he was already atop, wrestling the child across the room with a tickle of the ribs and ruff of red head and rub of what gets really read. You say it yet?

What?

You bet! And he was in for it fresh until in stitches, the pants pulled as far as the feet let them on him and his tormentor both.

Be a good boy now. Repeat what your mother said.

And still he never did until he was completely out of breath.

○ *Letters upon the light board*:
DEPENDENCE

Sentence upon the light board:
THAT DEPEND WHICH CAME FROM BEND BELIEVED THE END WAS.

○ *Letters upon the light board*:
SILENCE YET AGAIN

LOVER: Speak!
VOICE OF OBSERVER: [*coming from behind the man where she stands*] He doesn't.
LOVER: Talk to me!

86

VOICE: He doesn't want to.

LOVER: All right, be still then. You never do communicate properly!

VOICE: Abuse is not communication, he perceives.

LOVER: You'd rather hate!

VOICE: He is taught.

LOVER: I hate you for your silences, for all those refusals to treat me with decency.

VOICE: He is embarrassed by cliché.

LOVER: Night after night I greet you with a smile. I cook your food. I clean your dishes. And still you can't say anything but "Where'd you get those pair of pants?" or "You might have cleaned the lettuce better!"

VOICE: Dirt is trapped in his teeth.

LOVER: And if I try to talk about anything more than the weather—you put me down, dismiss what I'm saying, deliberately taunt me.

VOICE: Where is the cat? he wonders.

LOVER: And then, when I finally get sick and tired of such behavior, and complain just a little bit, you let loose with still more abuse.

VOICE: He sees by the clock it is nearly time to go to bed.

LOVER: You give nothing else—nothing that I need, that I want.

VOICE: He is embarrassed by generalities.

LOVER: I give you—patience at least. I ask about your day, your work. But do you ever show me you care? Do you know what I do even?

VOICE: He hates his mate's secrecy.

LOVER: And I when I try to describe what's happening to me, what I do, what I think, you dismiss everything. Tell me I'm a fool. A bore! A beast!

VOICE: Facts bore him too.

LOVER: And yet I listen to you. Night after night. How so-and-so said you are such a good dancer, that you still look good in tights. But in the flesh—you're a mess.

VOICE: The body no longer feeds his lusts.

LOVER: Oh, I'm willing—I've grown used to it—to put up with some abuse. But I can't tolerate your refusal to answer for what you've done.

VOICE: He cannot tolerate tears.

LOVER: Here we are again, me leaning over represented as a shrew, while you in some Zen position—which everybody recognizes is superior to a shrieking hen—wait until I'm worn out. And you who've fallen into a stupor by then can't comprehend what I go through.

The head wobbles with its snoring.

VOICE: Nor can he tolerate the truth.

○ *Letters upon the light board*:
LAUGHTER

Woman with the cat sitting on her lap

Honey, you gotta break it up or have it out. You can't keep him straddled cross the ax. Cut him down or the tree, but don't keep him in the noose!

I mean, if it was me I'd forget what you've been through. I'd let bygones be buried with the bones they begat. I'd let loose with the absolute delight of being here to see the daylight drift off into night. You know me, I'd kick up my heels if I didn't have such damn flat feet! If I had a body like you I'd fuck morning, noon, and around the moon.

But you gotta suffer. All you Jews. And you know I don't mean that to be prejudicial. Besides you didn't even know you was one—until I told you.

And, honey, you didn't have it half so bad as you might! As far as I can determine, you even liked it. You had a pretty cookie compared to the piece of gristle your mother had to chew.

Sure, you got a little confused. We all do. In getting fucked over you always get a little fucked up. But that don't mean you gotta run your scars under scalding water or put your ass in a block of ice.

People just got to learn to let happen what happens if it can't be stopped. I mean, you try. You try hard. You push a little harder, grimace a bit. But it just won't budge, back off! Get out of there, in fact, in case it rolls back.

But people like you sit around shaking their heads and beating on their chests like there was someone there to let them in. Baby, you're home already. And when that time comes you got to let out a sigh so loud it will fly from here to Hiroshima and back. And then you gotta get up and just dance or sing or tell a story or cross your eyes. And laugh.

Chorus dances a country dance to the calls of storyteller

> First enter an embrace.
> Then Efface.
> Put a hand into matter.
> Quick, hand the mater over.
> Meet one another at a brand new space.
> Lace your elbows round his waist.
> Gals bow to gals, guys to the floor.
> Once more.
> Erase.

○ *Letters upon the light board*:
MY SON

The voice of the woman at the well

You expect an explanation. I am mad, so they say, so I should not need give one.

Still, I am not angry, even though I killed myself. Do you really want me to explain?

To do so would make my act a result, not the cause it was to free you to forget. Forgetting, you shall see, is easy, natural as death. Living is the impossible thing! All that remembering!

They say it is selfish to put out the lights. But in the dark I lie, knowing everything must spin round your head each night. Mares whinny in the stable and the pale horse, left to field, noses ajar my door.

I want you to strew my ashes cross the nation, little by little, as you go from here to there, from no place to everywhere. I want to be spread along your path until there is nothing left.

In the War they wanted me to send Diane and you to the country. But I knew what that meant. Now, my wandering Jew, you can return to Brest and leave the bottle.

Complete blackout
Suddenly upon the screen a knife falls endlessly down down a well and out into a stream where stones are spun.

◐ *Letters upon the light board:*
MAN AND BOY

I lied to myself saying what I purposely forgot, perhaps not since lately I forget a lot. Such as the time I met, I don't recall his name, and we went, where I'm not certain, in some city, in some year. But I'm not sure of that since I now think I've begun to exaggerate a little about the past. But I did meet him, I believe, and fell in love, or least what I called love then—now I probably wouldn't describe it as such—and was all in a tizzy about seeing him again. Only I never did. He probably hid in the hall when I came to call or ran away out of town for fear I might come back, which as I promised, I did. So intense was I, he couldn't put up with it, I should imagine, or maybe he didn't enjoy the sex as much as I, although I can't remember any of those sensations now, but I recollect enjoying it then, or saying to myself the day after I did, that I really did find it so sensational, which was a word I just remembered I used back then. At the time it meant so much, but now it doesn't make much sense.

Or maybe he was murdered and the body dragged off. I never would have pictured that. He wasn't there so I just thought he doesn't dare or he doesn't care or he doesn't want to be with a person like me. But now I can call up all sorts of possibilities.

At any rate I never did try to visit him again in that house, in that town, in that year or any other one. And now I wouldn't even know his name if someone told it to me. And he wouldn't recognize me, nor, just as likely, I him.

But then, way back then, it made a sort of impression on me, clearly an impression which, despite my forgetfulness, I did not.

It was not the rejection—which is how I interpreted his not being there—but the fact that—if it was rejection—I so easily accepted it as such. Oh I was disappointed. I remember that I was young and I knew I could have my pick of almost anyone. But like most young folk I did not understand this potential. I did not know how powerful I had become. I could not even have imagined then that I might have scared him some. So I was blue for a day or two. But then I was not.

Now I so clearly understand, not me then, but him. He didn't want to be in love, didn't want to be involved with me. An hour with a young man was more than enough! A night was an eternity, dangerous at the very best. Like all young men I was out to change things or at least make them different. He didn't need to, didn't really want to alter anything. He was after nothing more than a respite from his wife, mate, mother, business life…. He sought only a sensation for the night. So my sensational night was, after all, nothing more, nothing less.

But that doesn't explain anything. Why I lied to myself and what about. But since I've forgotten I can't explain it. I can only report what I now think: that this man was already dead. And I knew that when I made love to him. And I knew that when I came back to see him he would have vanished without a trace. And I knew in that forgotten city, in that forgotten year, on that forgotten date, knew even before I knocked upon his door, that I was no longer the boy of the night before.

Now that I think of it, perhaps I never showed up. Perhaps someone—this imaginary man—waited for me at that door. And now I open it to see if the boy has kept his promise. And find he has not.

● *Letters upon light board*:
REFUSE

The MAN WHO RECALLS *walks down a New York Street. A* BUM *lies on the ground near a garbage container. The* MAN *walks by in a hurry. He stops, spins round, goes back and looks into the face of the drunken* BUM.

MAN: Monsieur Raison?
BUM: Huh?
MAN: Monsieur Raison, is that you?
BUM: Huh?
MAN: It's you, isn't it?
BUM: Who?
MAN: Monsieur Raison?
BUM: I don't speak Spanish.
MAN: How did you come….
BUM: Got a dime, a dollar'd be best.
MAN: I mean, how? Why you?
BUM: Who?
MAN: Here? You were always in control.
BUM: Can't help it.
MAN: It's the times I guess.
BUM: Yep. [*pointing to his blanket of newsprint*] The Times.
MAN: Can I help you.
BUM: A dime, dollar'd be better yet…
MAN: Here. Here, take it all.
BUM: Huh?
MAN: But tell me. Tell me, please, did you ever figure it out?
BUM: Who?
MAN: Yes. Who?

BUM: Yep. The Times.

MAN: Wasn't it. Terrible times.

BUM: Always is, has been.

MAN: Always will be.

BUM: Not for me. Today I got money.

MAN: Not so much there. I can get more.

BUM: Where?

MAN: Home.

BUM: Don't have one.

MAN: No. I guess you never did. The street was your home, wasn't it.

BUM: Street is.

MAN: Who did it?

BUM: Who?

MAN: Yes.

BUM: Did?

MAN: The murder?

BUM: You?

MAN: I told you it wasn't me.

BUM: Who?

MAN: The murderer. Did you ever find out?

BUM: Got another dollar?

MAN: [*feeling in his pockets, he uncovers a dime*] Here!

BUM: What do you want?

MAN: To know.

BUM: Oh.

MAN: Yes.

BUM: Oh .... I get it.

MAN: What?

BUM: You want me…

MAN: Yes.

BUM: Take me then.

MAN: What?

BUM: Can't be stopped. I'm drunk.

MAN: Do you want to go to my place?

BUM: If you can get me up.

The MAN *helps him up.*

MAN: Come. I need to know.

BUM: I won't help.

MAN: Get some coffee in you.

BUM: Gotta do it by yourself.

Walking with him in the direction opposite from which he'd come.

MAN: You know.

BUM: Yes.

MAN: I really loved him.

BUM: Who?

MAN: The corpse.

BUM: That too?

MAN: Not anymore.

BUM: So now it's me?

MAN: Yes. Yes.

Together they walk off.
Sounds of bombers, sword upon sword, a creaking board
Blackout

The MAN WHO RECALLS *is the Poet too. Before the curtain he speaks.*

MAN: These are not my memories. I have forgotten. Someone desires to live. And I do too, so that if I recall what didn't happen as if it did, mightn't it have, if I had lived…for example in France instead of where I won't even admit. Just a couple or maybe four years before I took my first breath, I also might have said: when I get out of this I will erase what has entered my head. Perhaps someone succeeded. And I now need recall what he needed to forget.

Curtain goes up on busy square where people go about their business fast. As the audience leaves the theatre, the following is read as a voice over:

The Walls Come True is based—in the broadest sense of the word—upon historical fact as recorded in the incredible philosophical-historical murder mystery of Claude Ricochet, *The Cross of Madame Robert.*

The story of the Robert-Croset families begins simply enough, in Brest, France, where a young Jewish girl grows up in poverty, the adopted child of a hard-working Protestant couple who run the local café. The young girl, Bette, is so completely dissatisfied with her lot in life, that she plans an escape, only to be raped in her last few hours in the city by a young man who works with her in the café. Despite the pleas of her guardians, Bette refuses to keep silent about the event, and the resulting scandal in this small provincial city forces the parents to marry her to a young man visiting on business.

The young girl is taken by her new husband, Henri Robert, to Villeurbane, a suburb of Lyon, where she spends a miserable summer bearing in late August a son, Henri-Claude. A daughter, Diane, is born the following year. And the children grow up together, leading outwardly normal lives that might fit the pattern of thousands of middle-class families throughout France. But this is only the beginning of a series of terrible events that ultimately reveal the Robert family clan to be as self-destructive and corrupt as the Julio-Claudians of ancient Rome or the Borgias of the Renaissance.

The summer is 1938 when the young Henri-Claude along with his close confident and playmate sister, witness the mental breakdown of their mother. The boy is quickly sent away by his "father" to boarding school in Switzerland. The child is terrified by the turn of events, and does poorly in his first term at school, a fact which Ricochet attributes not only to his alien surroundings but to the beatings and possible sexual abuse by his rector. Gradually the boy grows accustomed to his new life and eventually learns to love his school and friends, even tolerating his teachers.

Back in Villeurbane, meanwhile, Henri the elder mysteriously dies; and in the very next week, Bette, who has temporarily recovered her health, marries Pierre Narense, Robert's business partner and dearest friend. Villeurbane is also not without its scandalmongers, and the couple, with Diane in hand, are forced to flee the city to Paris, where they call for the return of the young Henri-Claude.

Once again life appears to go forward somewhat normally, despite recurrent "attacks" upon the mental health of Bette. But the German occupation of France quickly changes everything. As the Nazi forces come nearer and nearer to Paris Bette grows more and more frantic; the day of their march into the city, she takes her young son and hides him in an underground cave for two days and nights. When mother and son return to "the city of light," the Germans are completely in power, and the boy— who since the death of his father has refused to be called by his first name—is all the more startled for the transformation of his new environment.

The mother appears again to regain her health; but in actuality she lives most of her life in secret sexual encounters with the captors, even becoming the mistress of a high-ranking Nazi. Her husband becomes more and more distressed by his wife's behavior, following her into alleyways and houses of prostitution night after night, a harrowing journey which ends in his murder by a Gestapo group leader.

A closed inquiry follows, wherein it is revealed that Bette is Jewish by birth; but so entertwined has her life become with Vichy government officials, she is given her freedom in return for her agreement to send her children away—a euphemism for their extermination. Bette cleverly works out agreements with her husband's business associates to send her daughter to a convent in the United States and to sell her son to a wealthy Parisian judge.

The judge, Jean Croset, is known throughout the underworld of Paris as a sexual abuser of young boys; but Bette has either never heard the gossip, or, more likely, ignores the facts, and the boy is sent to live with Croset, who resides for the sake of appearances in a mansion with his own two sons and wife, who herself is involved with several young men of the upper class. Immediately, Croset takes the now pubescent boy as his lover. The wife, shocked by the conspicuousness of his actions, sends her sons to the very same school in Switzerland where Claude had been educated into the privileges of punishment and sex.

Ironically, the banishment of his sons only brings Croset closer to the boy, whom he now treats as son and lover; and a relationship soon evolves that is anything but what one might normally expect. Claude feels a deep love for his new "father/uncle/mate" and lives over the next two years what he later describes as the most joyful time in his life. Croset even manages to find a ballet teacher for his young charge, who is infatuated with dance.

But the world around him, as his mother once proclaimed, is utterly evil. The judge soon finds himself immersed in a scandalous trial, in which he is accused by the Vichy government of accepting bribes. Apparently, the case has been trumped up by the Nazi government in an attempt to ally themselves with the moral elements of Paris. In fact, the judge has begun to behave in months before as if public opinion could not touch him, taking his young lover with him to bars, dancehalls, and other places of low life, all which are brought forth in the Nazi press. So vicious are the attacks that the man commits suicide—at least that is how his death is described in the note he bears in his stiffened fist.

But the handwriting is not his, but that of the young Claude. Over the next few months, as the Allies move closer and closer to the outskirts of Paris, a detective—who has been on the track of Madame Robert for several years, uncovers facts that point to murder, a murder in which the boy, his mother, Croset's wife, and even his sons are suspects.

Soon after liberation, the boy understandably takes flight, arriving in New York City on VE day.

The Robert-Croset saga is one of almost labyrinthian coincidence. So it appears not to have surprised either Claude or Georges Croset, Jean's banished son, that they should meet by accident at a ballet school and fall desperately in love. For nearly five years they live in a tumultuous relationship, until Claude meets Patrice Croset, once again it appears by coincidence, on a Broadway corner. Patrice, the wife of Albert-Baptiste Croset (the other son of Jean, and Georges' brother) claims to have known Claude (who has legally changed his name to the American sounding Robert Williams) back in Villeurbane, and old wounds, fears and madnesses are reopened by her recollections. Patrice tells Robert (Claude) that he is Jewish, and things gradually begin to fall together in the tortured fragments of his memory. For the first time in his life, Robert suddenly begins to understand several of his mother's previously incomprehensible acts.

But Patrice is a fraud, eventually admitting that her husband has told her all about Robert and his family. She is actually an American, born and raised in Georgia. Oddly enough, Robert is more attracted to her after her confession, and they begin a financial relationship that surely shocked even the most decadant Manhattan denizens of the day. Using her husband as ticket to the most elegant of dinner parties and other events, Patrice introduces Robert to the Manhattan social elite, whom he, in turn, seduces, several times apparently bedding his hosts, wives and husbands, in return for money to keep silent.

Robert soon begins to display signs of madness not unlike his mother, alternating between periods of euphoric laughter and uncontrollable crying fits. To her credit, Patrice succeeds in imbuing him with a utterly pragmatic viewpoint of life. And it appears that Robert is moving towards a recovery when, on the night of August 4, 1950, he receives news of his mother's death by suicide.

The next morning he is found dead in his apartment, murdered by a tramp he picked up in the park. The bum confesses to the murder, but insists the victim had taken him to his apartment to force him into sexual contact. The trial, a long and complex one, reveals that Robert may have mistaken the bum for the detective who had followed his family for so many years throughout France, and had invited the tramp to his apartment in the hope that he had the answer to the murder of Monsieur Croset, the only human being—he purportedly told the tramp—he had ever loved.

My interest here was not in the plot of the lives—the chronology of which Ricochet adheres to faithfully—but in the series of seemingly never-ending horrors in which these two families found themselves enmeshed. From their youths to adult lives, mothers, sons, and daughters of both the Roberts and Crosets underwent a series of never-ending tortures. That their lives weave around one another and world events almost as a set of double-helixes so intrigued me that I found it necessary to put it into the form of a larger than life statement or opera.

Yet I was less interested in the larger events of plot than in the everyday experiences these families must have undergone. In that sense, I have focused my interest on everyday details—upon the language of mundane moments—rather than upon the larger currents. I have used these outrageous family histories as points of departure—not unlike Ricochet's own speculative reasoning—to meditate, linguistically, on the roots of destruction: hate, decay, fear, sexual depravity and tyranny.

And in this endeavor I have found it perfectly permissible to make changes in names (in actuality the detective was named M. Raisin, in English, Mr. Grape; but it was so close to the French raison, I could not resist) and even events. My goal was not historical accuracy but a linguistic reality that pulled the soap opera antics of these poor folk into the larger fields of the tragic and the comic.

The linguistic cadences of this piece, I eventually felt, created their own music—thus encouraging me to subtitle this work an opera. And this too is a fiction.

—DOUGLAS MESSERLI